COOLER | FASTER
MORE EXPENSIVE

COOLER | FASTER
MORE EXPENSIVE

THE RETURN OF THE SLOANE RANGER

PETER YORK &
OLIVIA STEWART-LIBERTY

Atlantic Books

First published in Great Britain in hardback in 2007 by Atlantic Books, an imprint of Grove Atlantic Ltd.

9 8 7 6 5 4 3 2 1

A CIP catalogue record for this book is available from the British Library.
ISBN 978 1 84354 677 1

Design by five twentyfive
Printed in Malta by Gutenberg Press

Atlantic Books
An imprint of Grove Atlantic Ltd.
Ormond House
26–27 Boswell Street
London WC1N 3JZ

TO SLOANES EVERYWHERE

Contents

INTRODUCTION

The Sloane is a beast almost unrecognisable from twenty-five years ago. Back then Sloanes were still nearly top of the pile despite the fact they rarely did anything remarkable: solicitors, the City (at one of the gorgeously named old Brokers), the Bar, publishing, the Army, auction houses, wine merchants, land agents, or farmers (Cirencester). Recognisable, familiar and dependable parameters secured the Sloane world. And all this was given a helping hand by the Sloane network of Old Boys, cousins and family friends. It was an enclosed monoculture.

Despite his gloriously predictable approach and thanks to the money-making efforts of his Grandfather, the Sloane felt he was King. In town he was known by most on his street, as they were largely (apart from the odd foreigner) other Sloanes he knew from the Country. Our Sloane was in good standing: he knew everyone at the local point-to-point (or he felt he did, especially after an afternoon in the beer tent). But unknown to our Sloane, around the corner trouble lurked.

Sadly, those certainties have gone. A lot has happened to change the Sloane world irreversibly. And in all those twenty-five years of social change what really mattered was the Big Bang. And Diana Princess of Wales. These two things hold the key to the Sloane's near destruction – and recent renaissance. After them just being a Sloane was no longer enough. A tornado hit the Sloane World: you could have a good name, a slightly famous grandfather, but it wouldn't be enough to make the cut. The situation was dire. The world was no longer interested in Sloanes. It wanted to know more about Celebrities: popstars, filmstars and entrepreneurs. Jane Procter became editor of *Tatler* and with that the 'Old Sloane Bible' changed. For ever.

JANE ON *TATLER*

'People think we're a toff's magazine. We're not. We are much more meritocratic than we used to be. We're only interested in titled folk if they are doing something interesting. We're interested in Jonathan Harmsworth because he's running 500 newspapers, not because he happens to be called Lord Rothermere. And we'd rather do the premiere of *Lock, Stock and Two Smoking Barrels*, because it is full of our friends.'

The *Tatler* reader, so it appeared, wanted to know about talented people, famous people, beautiful people. But why would anyone be interested in looking at pictures of people in magazines if they weren't people one had been at school with? asked Old Sloane.

SUCH A DIFFERENT WORLD

Since Diana Spencer married Prince Charles in 1981, the world has utterly changed. Then the heir to the throne married an aristocratic virgin. Today it is more than possible that our future Queen could be the daughter of a former member of cabin crew. So what changed the world?

THE BIG BANG

In 1986 the City was deregulated and for Sloanes London changed over night, with global investment banks, money and rewards. The Old School Tie didn't work. The American banks made it quite clear: they wanted the best men and women for the job, not just the person whose father had been at school with a descendent of the original banking family.

The £40,000-a-year Old Harrovians – the ones who had to take their socks off to count beyond ten – were blissfully unaware of this looming catastrophe. Employment on the basis of ability? It didn't cross their minds. And overnight the Old Boy Network upon which the Sloane world had relied started to unravel – though the Sloane took a few years to cotton on – and with it went the Sloane world, which fissured, splintering into thousands of impoverished shards. What little wealth some Sloanes might have had was annihilated by Lloyds a decade later. Big Banged and Lloydsized the Sloane was a shadow of his former self.

The Sloane needed funds. And in order to compete he had to up his game. The Young Sloane watched the flat on Pont Street being sold to finance the new roof in Gloucestershire. He watched as his parents faded into the countryside, both a lot poorer. He saw how smartly dressed, cut-throat Americans and Europeans in London were raking in the cash and Dammit! He wanted some. With billions shared out as bonuses in the City at the end of every year, is it any wonder that Sloanes have overcome their raft of inhibitions about money? He smartened up his act, got rid of his conspicuously frayed collars, updated his wardrobe and Turbo Sloane was born.

SINK OR SLOANE

But not all Sloanes rose from the ashes of the Big Bang like the Turbo. For many the changes were just too extreme. The city demanded talent, and this meant disaster for the less canny (basic model) Sloane. Up and down the country the lament was heard: 'Piers isn't going to keep up.'

As Sloane parents turned their attention to the country and their backs on cripplingly expensive London, for many the lesson learned was to survive on what one had. Well-cut suits last an age and if vulgarity was the price of wealth then the Turbo was welcome to it. Some things were priceless and for the Thumping Sloane the pace of change was a little too fast, the loss of pride unbearable, and the whole thing brash and American. Sloane ranks split further, and when one Thumping Sloane collected his boy from a Turbo's son's party he was left smarting as the child, comparing his friend's Rich List life to his own, asked 'Daddy, are you lazy?'

Yet the Sloane is a hardy beast. Whether Sloanes took it on the chin or went Turbo, stuck to Thumping ways or even rediscovered a rather lucrative version of the land as Eco Sloanes, the Networks were re-forming along new and interesting lines. As the old saying goes: you can't keep a good Sloane down.

DIANA

It was Diana who altered the Sloane map. In 1981, when she married Charles it would not have seemed ironic that this would be the woman to influence the Sloane world – after all she was (despite being an aristocrat) your archetypal Sloane: under-educated, nursery school teacher, pie crust collars. And she achieved every Sloane's Barbara Cartland dream: she married the heir to the throne.

So Di so Sloane, but it's surprising how she influenced the Sloane world, because she wasn't a Sloane hero at all in later life. Sloanes felt variously that she'd let down the Royal family, that she was silly and melodramatic – in those days bulimia was entirely unSloane – and that she cared too much about clothes. Plus, the Sloane's default setting (Queen and Country!) was to side with Charles. Nicholas Soames spoke for swathes of Sloaneshire when he called Diana 'mad'.

And when she died – appalling though it was – the Sloane wasn't quite sure how she felt about the very unEnglish mass sentimentality that followed. The Sloane might be reluctant to come out and say, it but actually she found the whole thing toe-curling.

And yet, *and yet* Diana got Sloanes to up their game. From the way they dress to the interest they take in grooming; from good works to glamour and interests in alternative therapies, it was Diana who created the new Sloane template. It was Diana who paved the way for Sloanes to become the sleek and glamorous celebrity loving do-gooders that they are today. In fact Diana was the pioneer for at least four new sub-categories of Sloane: the Sleek, Chav, Bongo and Party Sloane.

THE PROBLEM WITH KATE

God knows Sloanes hate snobs (See Rule 3). In fact, there's nothing like Mrs Bucket style snobbishness for demonstrating how utterly unSloane someone really is! But (and entirely secretly) the Sloane could not believe it when the newspapers announced the return of the Sloane Ranger traipsing in the footsteps of Prince William's girlfriend, Kate Middleton. Were they out of their minds? Kate of course seems a lovely girl and she's made a wonderfully loyal and dignified consort to Prince William. However the suggestion that she's a Sloane? Yes she went to Marlborough. Yes she wears Dubarry Boots. Yes, she gets the look absolutely right. Yes she's had a long term relationship with the heir to the throne. But being a Sloane is about so much more than that. One of her parents was an air hostess. There's no denying that people were absolutely vile about her family when she split up with William in April 2007, and none of it put Prince William's inner circle in a very good light: 'doors to manual' etc. It's just that Marlborough alone doesn't make an instant Sloane.

THE ROYAL FAMILY

Sloanes still believe in the Queen, but their views about the rest of the family have been sorely tested in the past twenty-five years. Except, of course, if they have been lucky enough to have actually met any of its members: 'Edward and Sophie are utterly charming,' proudly proclaimed one formerly cynical Sloane who spent a weekend with them. However, without the inside track most Sloanes have a fairly poor view of everyone except the Queen, the late Queen Mother ('Queen Elizabeth', as Thumping Sloane called her), who Sloanes adored, Prince Charles and Camilla – the Sloane loves Camilla and the boys. They approve of Zara – beautiful and brilliant with a horse; transfixed by her hideous accent. But that's largely it.

THE RULES

If Sloanes have changed so dramatically since 1982, what still makes them Sloanes? That's easy: scratch the surface and all the Old Sloane values are still there. Every Sloane knows the rules: which school, which car, where to ski, which clothes, which county, which postcode, which shoes, which vocabulary, which names and which bank.

THE RULES

1   The Sloane is not afraid of spiders, mice or ghosts – that's common.
2   The Sloane laughs at monogrammed luggage – or monogrammed anything – though secretly would love nothing more than to be a member of a family grand enough to carry off the whole monogrammed thing.
3   The Sloane hates a snob (an obvious middle-middle on the make) but she believes they are Quietly Right.
4   Compassion is an essential part of Sloane – what better way of reaffirming one's status than the right charity?
5   The Sloane is about the Country and gets involved at the County Show.
6   The Sloane went to the Right School like her parents, grandparents and even great-grandparents too. (It takes three generations to make a Sloane; two looks pushy).
7   The Sloane is on the lookout for tell-tale pronunciation: Ascot; forehead; 'either' (though there was a tricky moment when it emerged that Princess Margaret said 'ee-ther'. Things have since been resolved and the late Princess branded 'eccentric').
8   Mean. The Sloane can't help her natural setting: it's mean. The children eat Tesco Value range. But when it comes to her own food – particularly if she lives in town – it's more than likely to come from Waitrose.
9   The Sloane hates sentimentality or squeamishness: if you're going to eat it, you should be able to kill it. If you're sentimental about animals (except of course horses or dogs – the Sloane can't *bear* the idea of either in pain) you're not Sloane.
10 Shut up and get on with it!

SLOANE NO-NOS

1   Don't clink glasses when making a toast. Prince Charles doesn't clink.
2   Don't bring a bottle – you're not a student anymore
3   Don't lay the table with the spoon across the top of the place setting (there was some confusion when it turned out that the Queen Mother's table was always laid this way).
4   Don't say meal. It's lunch, supper, dinner or breakfast.
5   Don't say 'wealthy'. The word is 'rich'.

SPOT A SLOANE:

Reaction to the words Sloane Ranger is key to spotting a Sloane:
'Sloane Ranger?' [puzzled look] 'Do they really exist anymore?!'
'Sloane Rangers! Ha-ha!' [bemused look] 'I thought they died out years ago!'
Thanks largely to Harry Enfield and Tim-Nice-But-Dim, very few Sloanes under forty will admit to the name Sloane.

THE SLOANE DIASPORA

Sloanes have had a sizeable hole blasted through the centre of their world. In London they used to live in SW1, SW3, SW5, SW7, SW10. They might still have a toe-hold in SW10 but they have been expelled from great tranches of Sloane Land by the Bonus Boys: Russian oligarchs, American bankers and EuroTrash. The majority of the places over £3 million in SW-something go to 'Non-doms'.

There aren't many Sloanes left around Sloane Square. So those bastions of Sloanedom, the Sloane pubs, have been closing: perhaps most bitter was the end of The Phene Arms on Phene Street (catastrophic!). The passing of the Australian, and the nearby Shuckborough Arms, also came as body blows. Their re-opening as an expensive house for a plutocrat (the Australian) and a bakery (the Shuckborough Arms) hurt badly and showed that the people who ousted the Sloane from his natural habitat didn't mind paying £7 for a sandwich.

Displaced Sloanes have spread to parts of London they'd never have admitted to having heard of twenty-five years ago. They upped sticks first to Parson's Green and Fulham in the 1970s. In the 1980s they moved to Putney, Battersea (Prince of Wales Drive is the new Chelsea, says Sloane) Wandsworth and sideways to Baron's Court. And now to places that once completely spooked them: Shepherd's Bush, Acton, Balham, Tooting (the Heaver Estate – yes the Heaver Estate!), Streatham, Ladbroke Grove, Queen's Park, Kilburn, Brixton. The Sloane sighs: I love the East End but I never really go, it's much too far. In short it's an unlikely Sloane who lives in the East End. And it's fair to say Sloanes still have a thing about North London.

THE IMPORTANCE OF W10

For particular kinds of Turbo and Party Sloanes W10 is the centre of the world, especially the roads north of Ladbroke Grove tube station and even north of the Harrow Road. Particularly attractive to Turbo, Political and some Sleek Sloanes, however, are Oxford and Cambridge Gardens, St Marks and Highlever Road. Here you'll find Dave Cameron plus family; Freddie and Ella Windsor; Sabrina Guinness, Kinvara Balfour and Nick Jones. It has just the kind of mild edginess they love.

THE SLOANE HOUSE

It used to be easy. Done out in striped Laura Ashley wallpaper, with some Colefax and Fowler fabrics, a good neutral wool carpet with nice rugs on top and two cupboards on either side of the chimney breast which testified to the Sloane love of symmetry – everything in pairs. Dotted about the house would be significant clues to the last one hundred years of Sloane (portraits, Empire exotica, the odd elephant's foot, a scatter of ethic cushions), a nod to the Old School, with a First Eleven photograph in the lavatory. And of course, plain silver framed photographs of a grandfather shaking hands with the Queen Mother on those cupboards.

The decorative rules have changed completely. Twenty-five years of design coverage means Sloanes try harder and range further. The style could reasonably be described as Shabby Chic (though he'd hate that now – too 1980s – he would prefer 'eclectic') with a modest injection of mid-Century Modern pieces (picked up at auction) along with brown furniture from his grandparent's house.

Floors will be carefully polished and stained (salvaged) floorboards; walls will be Old White stone or even taupe, with perhaps one chocolate signature wall or a burst of curly-wurly wallpaper for fashion-conscious Sloanes. And on the walls there'll be some sort of modern art Sloanes have learnt to buy at art school shows in W10. Like everyone else, some big framed photographs.

New Sloanes think they've broken free from the old House Rules (things in pairs, old is best, chintz), but you still see a fair bit of traditional and transitional decoration in South London – the home of the more conservative younger generation Breeding Sloanes.

IN THE COUNTRY

Sloane parents will spend most if not all of their time in the country now – it's most likely that 'The Flat' has been sold. The old rule still applies: the only acceptable thing to do in the Home Counties is to be educated there. Eton, Stowe and all of the girls' schools are in the Home Counties. You just don't *live* in Bucks, Berks and Beds, rich and comfortable though they are. Surrey? It doesn't compute.

Counties for living in are Gloucestershire, Wiltshire. Oxfordshire, Northumberland, Dorset, Norfolk, Herefordshire and also increasingly Suffolk are good Sloane counties (though not Wales… there are no Dukes there). Scotland of course (though no accents). And Essex has some very Sloane parts.

NETWORKS

With the death of the Old Boy Network came the death of the Season. The fag-end of the Season went corporate and the Sloane no longer wanted to drive two hours into London to go to Ascot crammed with the common and corporately entertained, only to have to remain sober in order to drive back. (See Party Sloane). The Season was driven out of Town and back into the countryside. It went local and a new calendar sprung up around the County Show, local point-to-points, mini-Glyndebournish operas, parties and fundraisers.

The end of the Old Boy Network was a hard lesson for the Sloane to learn: It took him at least a decade to recover. However he adapted and – as Networks are entirely central to the Sloane – has established newer and more efficient ones which can work globally. (See Turbo Sloane).

New Sloane Networks demonstrate entirely vital Sloane family values (keeping others out). They've even made corners of the internet exclusive to Sloane: see FaceBook and asmallworld.com ('a private online community, which is designed for those who already have strong connections with one another') both of which you have to be 'invited' to join.

CHARITY

Sloanes have always found something very satisfactory about giving back (and confirming your status along the way). As well of course as being a great way to meet people and do a little discreet social climbing: for example, do something to save the planet and get Prince Charles on board. (See Eco Sloane).

It's also a great way for a Sloane with time on his hands to keep busy and visible while he's meeting likeminded people. Take Rugby Portobello Trust for example, a charity that lets rich Notting Hill people help poor Notting Hill Hoodies. It holds an annual quiz which is fiercely glamorous and fiercely competitive: and makes rich Sloanes feel good. David Cameron was captain of the Quiz for several years before he became leader of the Conservative Party: it's smart, fun and good for the social conscience and you don't actually have to meet any Notting Hill Hoodies. Perfect.

POLITICS

By nature the Sloane isn't a political beast. Naturally he feels happier when a friend is on the County Council (ideally its Chairman) but he doesn't see that has much to do with 'politics'.

Sloanes still overwhelmingly vote Conservative. That said they hated That Cretin Major to such a degree that things went tits-up in 1997. For the first time ever, many Sloanes didn't vote. And the few that did went Referendum Party; Lib Dem (those who fancied themselves 'intellectual'); and there were even a couple of desperate Sloanes who voted Green. Some modern Sloanes who lived in London and worked in the media actually voted for New Labour. Some Sloanes choose not to believe this: how could they be so easily fooled?

It's only when the Sloane feels his way of life is threatened that he stomps into action. This hasn't happened much. Until recently that is.

THE SLOANE ON NEW LABOUR

Sloanes despise Tony Blair more than any man alive. He stands for everything hateful: he's a Sloane Gone Off. He might have been New Labour but his background – Fettes, Oxford, the Bar – suggested that he'd know how to behave. But he didn't. He was really a middle management, left of centre type, married to a socialist, who betrayed his own kind to stay in power. That's how they see it.

Under Tony much of what Sloanes hold dear was attacked: hunting, smoking and farming, in a word, Freedom. Tony's Nanny State. The Sloane's favourite analogy is that no rules are needed in the messes of the smarter regiments in the army because people know how to behave. It's only in the fish and chip ones that rules are posted everywhere. Blair made this nation a fish and chip regiment; notices abound.

Under Blair, Sloanes will tell you, Britain became a reality TV country in which the lowest common denominator is celebrated as a national treasure. During his leadership you couldn't turn on the television without phenomenally ignorant dental nurse Jade Goody appearing. She was everywhere. The nation seemed to adore her. Sloanes didn't.

Foot and Mouth was a chronic mess achieved by people who'd never see a blade of grass in their life. And then came the ban on hunting. Suddenly the phlegmatic, law-abiding stalwart of his County was mobilised. In 2002 under the banner of Liberty and Livelihood 400,000 Sloanes marched on London (not all, mind, had to come in; many were already there).

Although not all marchers were Sloane, a fair number brought their friends and marched in plum or custard colour cords (folded into Hunter or Dubarry boots) topped with Barbours, shooting jackets and a reassuring acreage of tweed. Placards smacked of Jilly Cooper: 'For Fox sake, fox off Blair'; 'Towney Blair's got rid of more farmers than Mugabe'; 'We do not like being DEFRA-cated on'. Hard work the night before over some Jolly Good Red at kitchen tables all over Sloaneshire had certainly paid off.

On Tony's last night in office the world of Sloane echoed with the sound of corks popping.

THE SLOANE ON GORDON

Sloanes also have problems with Gordon. The whiff of unreconstructed socialism comes off him like steam off manure. During his time as Chancellor he taxed Sloane into oblivion. Case closed.

THE BROWN BURDEN

There's his refusal to raise the threshold on inheritance tax to something sensible like £2 million. When a Sloane dies the house – even the house that his been in the family for a century – has to be sold.

Council tax has doubled since 1997 making things rather desperate for the Retired Sloane at the Old Rectory

And then there's his refusal to abolish Capital Gains. He reckons he's saving the state money that should go on remedial work for mini-Jades.

THE SLOANE ON DAVE

On paper Dave's perfect: Eton, Oxford, Notting Hill; good green credentials and modern in an okay Sloaney sort of way. He even likes field sports, including stalking and hunting. And they say his constituency house in Chipping Norton smells of organic bacon sizzling on the Aga. His lovely wife Samantha Cameron, daughter of Sir Reginald Sheffield (Thumping Sloane) and Lady Astor (Turbo Sloane), is a credit, as is the number of Etonian MPs and advisers surrounding him. Furthermore his own impressive pedigree drops like a stone from William IV (via a royal mistress). So different from Mr Major (pooter), Willam Hague (weird), Iain Duncan-Smith (Clapham estate agent) and Michael Howard (spooky).

But there's something about Dave which makes the Sloane feel that he's been here before. Not least the fact that he's described himself as the 'Natural Heir' to Blair. He's always saying Blair-y things. About two years ago he was adamant about repealing the ban on hunting – he's been deathly quiet on that ever since. And that whole Grammar School debacle and his spineless U-turn were entirely Tony: sell your own kind down the river to keep the majority happy.

THE CAMERON CONUNDRUM

1 His insistence on being called Dave
2 His description of things as Huge
3 That whole Hug a Hoody rubbish: what a hoody needs is a bloody good hiding.
4 All that stuff about Bigging up Asda. Quite aside from what it means, Sloanes don't really feel at home in Asda.

THE FUTURE

There's no one the Sloane wants for PM. There's no one out there the Sloane can trust. Ideally the Sloane would like an acceptable 'One Nation' sensible Sloane with integrity and backbone who could lead the nation out of the mire, apply a firm hand and overturn the hunting ban. Or even someone unSloane: integrity and backbone would be a start.

It's not that the Sloane wants a return to Mad Bat Thatcher, but she did speak for the whole country when she tied that handkerchief over the tail fin of the British airways plane featuring one of those ghastly new designs in 1997!

But take Boris, at least you know where you stand with him. Eton, Oxford, yet so different from Cameron. With Bozza there's some fizz, some fire: he wouldn't let you down (unless of course you're his wife). But even then his adultery can be forgiven! There's just something so cheerful about it. But Boris for PM? Even backwoods Sloanes can see that'll take some banking now!

ON HOLIDAY

One kind of UK beach holiday is still very Sloane: try Brancaster in Norfolk, Rock in Cornwall and Croyde in North Devon. The Thumping Sloane will go to Scotland or the Hebrides. Turbo Sloane will holiday in the Caribbean for Christmas, St Trop or Ibiza for a couple of weeks in the summer – anywhere the party is. The rest of the Sloanes take summer holidays in Tuscany, Umbria, Andalusia or the South of France. And everyone goes to New York for a quick weekend and to Val d'Isère to ski. In fact holiday destinations are surprisingly unchanged since 1982.

ON SKIING

The Sloane adores skiing. Always has and always will. The Sloane year is just not complete without at least a week in the Alps. Because of this, some Sloanes are up in arms about Global Warming and bad-snow reports are greeted angrily: 'Bloody global warming!'

Val D'Isère is still a favourite spot (Val Sloane Square) as is Courchevel (Courche). And at both these places the onlookers will be greeted with the overwhelming sight of pink-faced Sloanes, unmistakable in their cufflinks, whistling down the mountainside. Other Sloane spots include Meribel, St Anton, Klosters (where a cousin of the Palmer-Tomkinsons' runs his bar – in nearby Davos), Verbier, Zermatt and Lech.

G'staad is just too Euro and just too expensive. As for the true Thumping Sloane, he swears he had his best ever powder-day at Scotland's Aviemore.

CAN YOU GROW YOUR OWN SLOANE?

In the Old Days, a Sloane was a Sloane and that was that. Today, the divide between the have-cash and the have-none is vast. In some areas of Sloane this makes absolutely no difference: a Sloane is still a Sloane. In others however, particularly when bringing up Baby, the divide shows. But one fact remains stubborn: even if you stick to every single word of the Sloane code for bringing up your child you can't make a Sloane; that takes at least three generations. (See Rule 6).

SLOANES: THE EARLY YEARS

GIVING BIRTH

Sloanes with Cash and Sloanes without Cash both tend to give birth under the guidance of the NHS. There's something rather un-brave, perhaps a little Posh 'n' Becks, about spending a bundle on going private, especially as the net result isn't going to be any different. The Sloane is similarly unimpressed by the pre-booked Caesarean. And most important, that 6 or 10k could be put to much better use i.e. towards the all important school fees. After all, the hospital into which you are born has no bearing on your life, unlike your school which counts for pretty much everything.

NAMES

Basic Sloane rules still apply: girls' should end in 'a' and boys' should be after kings. The rules are bent as fashions come and go. A recent trend in Sloane naming was the Victorian serving classes: Alf or Lily; Betty, Millie, Ruby, Jack, Bert, Joe and Fred. Local attachments amongst Sloanes are also common: there's currently a deluge of Graces in the Notting Hill area – most of the girls at Pembridge Hall have the middle name Grace (best as a middle name, what if she grows up fat?).

GODPARENTS

The Sloane is an ambitious parent and godparents are crucial. A Sloane child will have four: two men and two women and the Sloane parent is ruthless in his pursuit of the rich, the titled, the successful, the Royal. As godparents, obviously royalty is best, but failing that, rich with excellent contacts makes a good second choice. Godparents can make or break a Sloane: having Prince Charles as a godparent did Tom Parker Bowles no harm. Would David Cameron be where he is today without for the Conservative MP for Lewes, who did the godfatherly thing and gave Cameron three months work experience after school? The right godparents are about contacts, contacts, contacts.

NANNY

These days the live-in nanny is more often for celebrities, rich Americans and Euro Sloanes (and of course, Turbo Sloanes). At 30k a year Norland Nannies are rare in Sloane households: they tend to be more something that celebrity (Mick Jagger employed a Norland) or Royalty (Prince Andrew and Princess Anne both had Norlands) chooses. Plus, for most Sloanes, with their brown uniforms and tight buns, they're a bit stern.

If a Sloane does have a live-in nanny, it's grand to have an English nanny and grandest of all is to have one's own childhood nanny brought down from the Lake District and now installed in SW6. The Fillipino nanny is making inroads into Sloane households but as a general rule Sloanes aren't that keen on *staff*: someone to help out, yes, an au pair who gets board and lodging, but mainly someone who can muck in with the family. It's also quite common for the Sloane in Nappy Valley (Shepherd's Bush, Clapham, Battersea or Balham) to share a nanny with another nearby Sloane. The bottom line is that nothing, but nothing, beats a mother who's there for her brood. Rupert was completely messed up by going off to school at seven and a generation on, the evolved Sloane won't let that happen to her own. She's a brilliant mum on nanny's day off – resourceful, patient, imaginative. Once breakfast's over she'll set about turning cereal boxes into trucks to keep two-year-olds amused at the same time as answering the

telephone and running, from home, her embryonic mail order business.
And where to find one's nanny? If word of mouth hasn't unearthed anyone
suitable, there's always *The Lady*.

NURSERY

Pre-school activities are very often the preserve of the cash-rich time-poor Yank
or Euro Sloane in London. The Sloane might be rather snobbish about the
ambitious contingent in London whose child's life is a ruthless round of
improving ballet, ju-jitsu, judo, poetry, French classes and painting. Rather than
joining the investment banker at Gymboree in Chelsea Harbour at the weekends,
the canny Sloane is much more likely to be the person running the venture.
(See Turbo Sloane.)

PREP SCHOOLS

It has dawned on Sloanes – it has only taken about 120 years – that seven is a
somewhat brutal age for a child to be sent off to school. These days Sloanes are
coming around to the idea of waiting until a boy is thirteen and a girl, eleven
before packing their trunk. Despite this, your prep school is important and often
influences which school you end up at: many Sloanes will follow their prep
school friends onto their next school. Day prep schools are a booming market –
especially in rich London.

Notting Hill Sloanes go alongside the children of international celebrities to
Pembridge Hall and Wetherby. Other London choices include Eaton House,
Falkner House and Garden House School which has a proud new location on the
Kings Road at Duke of York Barracks. Outside London Sloane choices include the
Dragon, Cothill House, Ashdown House, Godstowe, Sunningdale, Summerfields,
Prestfelde, Packwood Haugh and, most Sloaney of the lot, Ludgrove.

SCHOOL

The single most important factor in any Sloane's life: school. It's best to go where ones father and grandfather and even great-grandfather went. Failing that, the bottom line is that you can't be a Sloane if you didn't go to the right school. It's a rare Sloane who can get away with a Grammar School education. This has been a terrible blow to Sloanes as not all recovered from Lloyds and each child's schooling will cost in the region of £40,000 in pre-tax earnings per year (and that's before uniform, kit, books and extras are accounted for). And so it follows that today, most of the once exclusively Sloane schools are no longer entirely Sloane: since the Big Bang, End of Term has stopped being a shambles of dog-haired covered estate cars and Land Rovers. These days it's a parade of shiny tint-windowed four by fours, picnics by Fortnums and even helicopters. The Sloane Factory schools have changed from predominantly Sloane to overwhelmingly Cash.

Ampleforth:	Amplewealth
Bedales:	Bit too artsy celebrity!
Benenden:	Helicopters and cash
Charterhouse:	Big on sheep
Cheltenham:	Euro-royal
D'Oeverbrooks 'Dovers':	Retakes
Downe House:	Enid Blyton
Downside:	Euro trash
Eton:	Think they're God's Gift
Godolphin & Latymer:	Square
Harrow:	A Harrow social is always carnage
Heathfield:	Party!
Marlborough:	Way out!
Millfield:	For those with authority issues
Queen's Gate:	Who cares?
Radley:	Rugger
Rugby:	Very rich
Sevenoaks:	Euro

Sherborne:.. Sporty

St Edwards: .... Naughty

St Mary's Ascot: .... Sloane central!

St Swithuns: .... Take their lax too seriously

Stowe:.. Sturdy boys and party girls

The Lycee: .... French

Tudor Hall: .... Very country – they despise London

Wellington:.. Soldiers with acne

Westminster:.. Bright but not shiny

Westonbirt:... very Gloucestershire

Winchester: .... Geeks – they care more about A-levels than girls

Wycombe Abbey: .... Brains over Beauty

THE GAP YEAR

The Sloane emerges from school, post-A-levels, bubbling over with tales of *wicked* pranks: a brilliant laugh on muck up day, for example, might have been putting the headmaster's house on ebay – it was so random – or turfing the 6th form common room! And then comes the real work: sorting out the all important Gap Year. Twenty-five years ago it just didn't happen. Now it's a rare Sloane who doesn't take a Gap Year: Gap years are immense!

Since they became a big thing to do, Sloanes haven't veered much form the original path: twenty years ago Sloanes who did take a Gap Year might have stacked shelves at the GTC and then gone off to study History of Art in Florence at the British Institute. The Sloane still does that (albeit at the GTC's new and somewhat less satisfactory location on Symons Street). Other Sloanes' idea of heaven could well be doing a working Season at their favourite ski resort. Most don't go back: it's something of a shock and the Sloane chalet girl – if she does stay the distance – will spend many nights on the phone in tears to her parents: 'It's bloody slave labour!'

CHALET GIRL

The would-be Sloane chalet girl leaves school to go direct to Prue Leith's cookery school where she'll spend the summer (three months) learning how to bake cakes and other soul-warming foods suitable for skiers (stews, casseroles, pies) as well as all important skills including how to cook at high altitudes (it ain't as simple as it sounds). The Prue Leith course will even help to finalize a position at a resort for the fledgling chalet girl when she leaves. From there to Val d'Isère (a top choice) where she'll mingle with other chalet girls and Sloane boys in the Gap Year uniform of gel-spiked hair and Jack Wills clothing. Failing Val, she'll go to Courchevel (1850 of course, anything below this is rather second-rate).

And so her time as a 'Seasonaire' begins. From the end of October until May, she'll be expected to cook and clean for holiday makers. She'll be allowed to ski between 10 a.m. and 3.30 p.m., when she has to be back at the chalet to serve cake. The pittance that she's paid just about covers her alcohol. At the end of six months she comes home with panda eyes (the deeper the contrast, the cooler the Seasonaire), and the dreaded Chalet Girl Bum (apparently inevitable, no matter how thin the chalet girl before arrival, thanks to the lager and the food).

More than anything the chalet girl dreads Saturday (change over day – the whole chalet has to be made spotless in preparation for new guests) and February, which is notorious for 'Mid-Season Blues' when the girl is bound to get 'a ghastly group of pikies who got the holiday cheap and have no idea how to behave'. To this end, all experienced chalet girls recommend working for only two companies: Scott Dunn and Mark Warner, both of which specialize in offering holidays to a good Sloane clientbase (i.e. people who know how to behave).

Alternatively, boys might decide to qualify as an instructor: if only to don a jacket that greatly increases his chances of pulling.

Other Gap Year jobs include answering the phone in the company belonging to your most successful godparent, particularly in PR (heaven!); at a children's clothes shop in SW3 or SW1 (sooo boring!); as a waitress for the Admirable Creighton or At Your Service (terrible!) or at the till in Tiffany's (unbelievable! You're not allowed to sit down!)

And then it's time to travel: for maximum kudos the Sloane goes to India spending a lot of time on the beach in Goa doing drugs at various festivals. Other Sloanes might do time at an orphanage or animal sanctuary before going off travelling. If the Sloane goes to Africa, it's likely he'll becomes obsessed with it. Africa – Botswana, Kenya, Mozambique, Malawi, (certain parts of) South Africa – changes Sloanes. The majority of Gap Year Sloanes stick to the Beaten Track though: two months in Australia and then home via Thailand, Vietnam and Cambodia. But especially Thailand.

It's also during this year that the Sloane will spend time marking himself out as an *individual*: he might pierce an eyebrow or tongue. She might get a tattoo (a dolphin, flower, or gecko on the wrist, nape of neck, or ankle). And all will certainly return with arms weighed down with copper bangles, friendship bands and elephant hair bracelets.

UNIVERISTY
After the Gap Year it's time for the Sloane to go, wiser, older and possibly thinner (if he spent time in a third world country), to university. The main thing to have changed since Diana's day is the fact that the Sloane now sees fit to educate his daughters. A quarter of a decade ago it wasn't a given that girls went to university. Now it's unusual for them not to: 95 percent of Sloanes go to university.

TOP TEN SLOANE UNIVERSITIES:

Oxford (for the bright. Not Cambridge – that's for dweebs)

Oxford Brookes (Sloane Heaven)

Edinburgh (a huge percentage of Eton ends up at Edinburgh)

Newcastle (both the University and the former Polytechnic – now the University of Northumbria – are packed with Sloanes having a reet laugh on the Tyne, although some get beaten up)

Bristol (a good Sloane contingent keeps tension with the locals high)

University of the West of England, UWE, (Also in Bristol, though here it's ALL Sloane)

Durham (still Sloane-heavy)

St Andrews (back up there now that monarchy-hunting Americans have finished their degrees)

Please Note: Sloanes can be found in History of Art departments at every institute for further education in the country.

THE FULLY-GROWN SLOANE

Once the fledgling Sloane (found hungover, fresh from bed, ordering restorative Bloody Marys for himself and his friends at four o'clock on a Saturday afternoon in Foxtrot Oscar) has been schooled and Gapped, he or she will find their way into one of the categories that form this book. She might pursue a career in reality television (the Chav Sloane), he may go all out to save the world (Eco); or she could go stratospheric (Turbo). Whichever path the new Sloane chooses, they've all come from and they're all heading back eventually to the same reassuring, solid Sloane root.

HATCH, MATCH, DISPATCH

CHRISTENINGS

Sloanes don't really like Naming Ceremonies: they're rather foreign or arriviste, short on tradition, along with Baby Showers and other American imports. The Sloane is all for tradition, particularly tradition which highlights one's standing in a community. In other words a Christening is best done in the village church where you and all your forbears were christened, married and buried. And the preference would be to have the same presiding vicar who christened you. And even if you're a Sloane who married out (American; Euro; plutocrat) when it comes to *these* things, tradition must prevail.

N.B. The Sloane protests loudly against the current fashion for sharing a church and vicar on the occasion of a child's baptism: it just doesn't feel right!

MARRIAGES

Sloanes still like to marry Sloanes. The women marry in their late twenties or early thirties and the men in their early to mid thirties. Any sooner is considered a little odd. The norm is to marry someone met in the country, at Annabel's or, failing that, to marry a friend from university.

Currently it seems that Sloane women are having a tough time finding someone to marry: Sloane men are marrying out. They're marrying Americans or South Americans, leaving some female Sloanes on the shelf. 'There's just no one to marry!' exclaims one successful thirty-two-year-old Party Sloane. She says the blame rests squarely with American women: 'they've watched *Gosford Park* and they're coming over here to marry posh British men: my brother married one! We never see him any more. It's a nightmare!'

When eventually the Sloane does marry, the wedding is held in the church in which she was christened: 'I Vow to Thee My Country', 'Jerusalem', a verse from *Song of Solomon* and then it's back to the house, to a marquee on the lawn, to champagne and the works: June, salmon, speeches, tears and summer berries. Hurrah!

FUNERALS
See Christenings: the drill is much the same.

SMART TO BE SLOANE
These days it's truly smart to be a Sloane. Why? *Four Weddings and a Funeral* was crucial, in particular Hugh Grant. The world fell in love with Hugh Grant. At last there was a Sloane who wasn't a creepy pervert (Uncle Monty from *Withnail and I*). *Four Weddings and a Funeral* was a film about Sloanes starring Sloanes for Sloanes – it was funny and real and honourable and romantic and cleverly bumbling. And all the extras wore their own morning coats (potatoes wear jackets) and the world adored them. Hugh became the first Sloane pin-up and the Sloane is now in demand as a National Treasure.

We've got Sloane politicians: Boris, David Cameron (he's modern and smart), Zac Goldsmith, George Osborne. Sloane popstars: James Blunt (he lost his 'o' just a few years ago); Harry from McFly; Charlie from Busted. We've got Sloane comedians: Marcus Brigstock, ('Yes, I'm posh… there I was in Verbier'); Xander Armstrong. We've got Sloane actors: Rupert Everett, Damian Lewis, Rosamund Pike. And the nation is inundated with Sloane models (see Sleek Sloane). These days it's more than okay to be a Sloane: they're entrepreneurial; they're bright; they know everyone they need to know; they're confident; they're even sleek. And they're definitely cooler, faster and more expensive.

ECO SLOANE

Meet
Ben

Ben, 36, lives with his wife Tara, 32, and their baby, Uma, on the upper two floors of a house in a square at the north end of Ladbroke Grove. He was the first in the square to attach a wind turbine to the roof of his house – and the first to take it down again: contrary to the information on the DTI's wind measuring website, this part of West London does not boast enough air-movement to supply a household's electricity let alone generate the anticipated surplus that Ben was looking forward to selling back to the national grid. However, at least their friends – and neighbours – know (and how they know!) that they've tried.

Planning permission has come through for their solar panels which will go up next spring, thereby providing hot water and halving household energy consumption in winter. 'Oh, good,' said their downstairs neighbour, some kind of policy adviser to the shadow cabinet who was a couple of years below Ben at school. 'I wasn't sure how keen I was on having a windmill on top of the house!' Ben and Tara have dined out on this for several weeks: isn't the Opposition Party supposed to be about the environment?

Ben and Tara met at a fundraiser organized and hosted by a rather well-known Eco Sloane. Back then Ben had been invited in his capacity as well-paid employee of an American bank (which happened to be looking for a 'Green-wash'). And it was there that he underwent his Damascene conversion. Among ageing rock stars and Green-friendly supermodels, among plutocrats and cottage garden hollyhocks, on a wonderful stretch of lawn somewhere on the River in Richmond, Ben met his wife. An ethereal barefoot creature, who'd known their Eco host since birth (her mother's organic farmstead abuts his parents' rather impressive estate), Tara offered him a glass of elderflower champagne. And Ben realized that the future was Green. He took Tara's number and also the number of a young Eco buck who was in the process of setting up a Green Fund specializing in carbon off-setting, something about which Ben had never heard.

Tara offered him a glass of elderflower champagne. And Ben realized that the future was Green.

That was three years ago and now Ben and Tara
fly the hemp flag higher and with more
panache than anyone they know. Ben has
learned a lot from his wife and can be
heard these days saying things like:
'Simply put, our grandfathers' battle
was the Second World War; ours
is Climate Change.'

And the fund has surpassed all
expectation. They have an
office on the penultimate floor
of the Gherkin (one of the most
environmentally sound buildings
in London, 'It uses half the power
a similar tower would typically
consume', as Ben never tires of
telling visitors, 'thanks to its natural
ventilation system, its passive solar heating
and its maximization of daylight.') Ben is uneasy
about the number of transatlantic flights he has
to take for work, but justifies them as a means to
an environmentally responsible end. He always
offsets his own flights – after all, he laughs, if he
doesn't do it, who the hell will?

Tara's got her name down for an allotment but, to be
perfectly honest, she is relieved that the waiting list is still years long – where would
she find the time? With Uma and her commitments to the Sorted Baby, the
environmentally sound mother's advisory service which she co-founded with the wife
of another rather well-known Eco Sloane, she just doesn't have a minute. In the
meantime, the family makes do very nicely with their weekly organic veg box.

Tara is something of an environmental pioneer: she's sourced a new energy-efficient light bulb which doesn't make one feel as if one's back in the dingy 1950s and it's now illuminating the hallways of all her friends. She's also pioneered her set's move into James Jeans – she'd die without LA-based Seun Lim's organic denim! She teams them with the odd item from the Cross: Temperley or some such and with something fair trade from People Tree (and yes, she was buying from them long before Sienna Miller took up the baton).

Uma wears hemp and organic cotton and started off in proper nappies but is now in the biodegradable variety. (The never-ending washing was beginning to grate on Tara's nerves and it made her question how energy-efficient real nappies actually were, what with the tumble-dryer and washing machine being in constant use).

Ben suspects that he probably should be wearing hand-me-downs and clothing from other renewable sources like some of the other high profile Eco Sloanes, among them his co-founder in the fund who always wears suits which were made for one of his notoriously glamorous uncles who died in a helicopter crash in Kenya in the 1970s. Ben doesn't know anyone whose hand-me-downs he'd be happy to wear. The trouble is, where investors are concerned, Savile Row talks and as the fund still requires investors, Ben felt compelled to invest in a couple of very good suits. As he tells everyone, the linings are organic silk.

When he isn't away on business, he, Tara and Uma make a point of leaving early on Friday – just after lunch – in order to hit the A40 in their Honda Prius before the traffic gets hideous. Tara drove a G-Wiz before and while she was pregnant – she was one of the first in London to get one – but it's just impractical with a baby, plus she

Ben has learned a lot from his wife and can be heard these days saying things like: 'Simply put, our grandfather's battle was the Second World War; ours is Climate Change.'

Ben has always known that green is his favourite colour. In fact it's every Sloane's default colour. Green is the land and land, in this country anyway, is invariably grand.

found it upsetting when, for the second time, the kids from the local estate lifted it onto the pavement and tipped it over – at least, that's what she presumed happened.

And if she was being entirely honest, the car was a total nightmare to charge (seeing as they live in a second floor maisonette) and she never felt entirely comfortable going milk-float slow uphill.

At weekends, the family looks forward to time spent in their own quarters at Tara's mother's Queen Anne farmhouse on her organic smallholding in Oxfordshire, where she's currently experimenting with clover as a means of returning nitrogen to the soil. Tara's mother was ecological before they even invented the word for it! And it's here that Ben is heavily involved, along with the entire family of Eco Sloanes whose estate lies next door, with the local campaign to stop 870 homes going up on greenfield sites just two miles from Tara's mother's farm.

Ben's single regret in going Green is that he's had to give up his Range Rover. There are upsides, however: he's now friends with people who are household names and his name is Green the Sloane world over. To this end he's written several pieces for various ecological magazines including one about his experience of domestic wind turbines in London. In the course of his research he discovered that South London – Crystal Palace, in fact – was the best place in the capital for wind-generated electricity: but you'd have to be quite a committed Eco Sloane to move down there!

Long before he went Eco – which he's been since he was knee-high – Ben always knew that green was his favourite colour. In fact it's every Sloane's default colour.

Green is the land and land, in this country anyway, is invariably grand. In fact the UK is the only country in Europe where this is the case, mostly because there's relatively little of it to go around. And so Ben and Tara's London circle echoes with the familiar refrain: 'Are you in the country this weekend?'

If Ben were to voice a wish in a public environment – let's say a fundraising luncheon at Highgrove – it might be that travelling by aeroplane be banned. His real wish is for a nice traditional chunk of land not too far from London on which to run a hobby-farm and experiment with organic veg, rare breeds and a clutch of high-visibility, roof top wind turbines – this last, of course, strictly only at weekends. Also, in keeping with his understanding of the rhythms and traditions

Ben and Tara's london circle echoes with the familiar refrain 'Are you in the country this weekend?'

of the countryside, and in sympathy for the cause, he would probably run a shoot and he would certainly allow the hunt across his land.

Ben's wish would also most likely include, in common with the wishes of many of those in his circle, the trading in of his half-house at the north end of Ladbroke Grove for something stucco in Phillimore Gardens. And if the fund keeps going the way it has, it might not be too long before Ben's wish comes true. In the meantime anyway, and even without the farm, Ben feels he's doing his bit: the Eco Sloane is about so much more than getting one's hands dirty. Green is a vital means of distinguishing the New Sloane from the merely rich.

Sloane in the Country

1. Gloucestershire

2. Dorset

3. Norfolk

4. Hampshire

5. Northumberland
(a county in which there are the most – and the least – Sloanes. There's nobody there, but those who are, are largely Sloane.)

N.B.: The Home Counties are for school.

ECO SLOANES –
THE BACKGROUND

A group in some ways similar to the Eco Sloanes appeared in the late nineteenth centry when prominent 'thinkers' and aristocrats formed a salon – the Souls, later the Coterie. The Souls were sensitive, artistic, evolved and *intense*, and they railed against the rise of the middle class, the subsequent spread of the suburbs and literacy, and the appalling taste of the new Victorian bourgeoisie. In effect, they became a stick with which to beat back the mass of the growing middle class and keep down the upwardly mobile Victorian.

Green is the stick with which the Eco Sloane can beat the vulgar rich in a country where, increasingly – since 1986, anyway – money talks. The past twenty years or so may have seen the Sloane shunted from his natural habitats of SW1 and SW3 and from the better houses in the country. Russian oligarchs, footballers, David and Victoria Beckham may have money; Elton John might have even more money; but still the Sloane has his past, his culture and good instincts as well as his green hinterland to distinguish him from the others.

Anything not Green smacks of low moral and low educational tone: gas-guzzling cars and children raised on fast foods in disposable packaging, in front of reality TV. Would Jade Goody, Victoria Beckham or Paris Hilton take the train? Would Victoria trade in her 4x4 for an electric about-town plastic car with a top (downhill) speed of 40 mph? Would any of them use energy-efficient light bulbs, try wind turbines, or grow their own veg? Exactly!

It's not just moral tone, there's something else here too: Green is about conservation which suggests having something to conserve. It's about wealth beyond one generation which again elevates the Sloane above new money. As any honest Sloane knows, it takes just three generations to make a gentleman. And once that gentleman is made, it's important to keep pretenders out. At a garden party in Notting Hill last summer to celebrate the launch of a book, the mother of a contemporary of Ben's at Eton, a Sloane with a surname familiar on the High Street, was heard summoning guests to the far end of the garden with cries of, 'You must see this!' She was intent on pointing out a 'carbuncle' which a neighbour – 'the banker!' – had attached to the side of his house. The fact that her fortune was down to her great-grandfather who was the owner of a late-Victorian printing business, was irrelevant as was, of course, her celebrated marriage to a man whose grandfather started a high street store.

Everyone must start somewhere: while Americans love instant success the Brits, and Sloanes in particular, remain wary of it. Eco gives them back the edge.

THE PRINCE OF WALES: KING OF GREEN

How things have changed. Can it really only be two decades ago that the *Sun* derided the Prince of Wales as 'a loon with his thoughts' and the *Mirror* voiced its concern at the possibility of a monarch sitting 'cross-legged on the throne wearing a kaftan and eating muesli'? Is it really only twenty years ago that a writer in the *Guardian* – yes, the *Guardian*! – ridiculed the Prince's idea for a bottle bank outside Buckingham Palace and wondered if this 'strange machine' would lead to the transformation of the palace into 'allotments with windmills creaking away in an attempt to provide electric power and composting lavatories…'?

He may only be a prince but he is certainly the King of Green. That 'wacky' man is leading the charge and hordes of Eco Sloanes are getting into line behind him to sound the battle cry. Green is grand. And rumours that the Prince floats through an incense-infused Highgrove naked beneath a simple cotton kaftan, (and provides similarly loose kit plus Moroccan slippers for guests), has been enough for the Eco Sloane to consider the practicalities of implementing similar schemes at home.

HOW TO GET THE HIGHGROVE LOOK

INCENSE: from pure-incense.com. Or if you're after something French and less 'authentic', try Terre d'Oc, 26 Marylebone High Street, W1 (020 7486 0496) and 184 King's Road, SW3 (020 7349 8291).

KAFTANS: from kaftans-direct.co.uk. For the real deal, try this reasonably priced web based, mail order kaftan store. Choose between batik, plain, velvet or carnival. The more style-conscious Eco Sloane might find something from Antik Batik, Anya Hindmarch or Aspara more fitting.

SLIPPERS: Kazzbar at craftmarketcorner.co.uk for beautiful Moroccan slippers in a range of colours including a prince-like silver. From £24.99. Or order your pair at half the price from maroque.co.uk.

CANDLES: from the Candle Shop, 50 New Kings Road, London or even better, the Organic Pharmacy, 396 Kings Road from £39.95 each. They are 'handmade with natural plant and bees wax. That means no soot, no petrochemicals and of course no artificial fragrances.'

THE HEAVENLY HOST

The children of the ruling classes have always dominated the green movement. It has traditionally been seen as an indulgence of the privileged: a lord ran Greenpeace; a baronet (who turned down the baronetcy) started Friends of the Earth; one particular marchioness has a very public finger in pretty much every Green pie; and the UK's leading and most vociferous anti-globalization campaigner is the son of a super plutocrat who owed his fortune to Campbell's global canned soup empire. Whereas just a decade ago, these kinds of people might have been seen as slightly off-centre they are now where it's at. These are the people the nation wants to hear from: the impossibly privileged, the impossibly rich, and often – for some reason – the impossibly good-looking.

Ben likes to think of himself as being one of them. He has not met the Prince of Wales yet, but he and Tara were at a party last summer held in honour of the Asian elephant, and the Prince and the Duchess of Cornwall were there that night too.

Zac Goldsmith:

- Wears second-hand clothes
- Rolls his own cigarettes
- Is pro-hunting
- Is anti-nuclear
- Is a Tory candidate for Richmond Park
- Thinks plastic should be banned
- Travels by train
- Shuns supermarkets (when in London he takes a weekly organic veg box (Abel & Cole), shops at Chelsea Farmers' Market on Sydney Street, and for cheese goes to Neal's Yard)
- Is on a mission to change the world

THE ECO SLOANE PIN-UP

The Eco Sloane has one hero (not counting Prince Charles who is of course a class apart) and that's Zac Goldsmith, the Old Etonian editor of the *Ecologist* and London's most glamorous, most handsome, richest eco-warrior. Eco Sloanes love nothing more than to be invited to one of his fundraisers and, with this in mind, they'll contribute to his magazine, they'll praise him publicly and they'll work tirelessly for his pet causes.

Who is Zac?

By dint of being the son of a capitalist (Sir James Goldsmith) whose empire spanned the globe, who had three private jets (including one Boeing 757 converted into a personal pleasure dome), whose fortune came from a variety of (many environmentally questionable) concerns including Ambrosia Creamed Rice and Bovril (numerous ranches and abattoirs across Argentina) and who was renowned for the commercial ruthlessness displayed in his hostile takeover of Goodyear Tyre and Rubber Company, the third largest manufacturer of rubber in the world, Zac is estimated to have a fortune of some £300 million.

More handsome than the sun, richer than Croesus, married to an exquisite model, with a townhouse in Chelsea and an organic farm in Dorset. On top of all that, he wants to give something back. Is it any wonder that everyone wants to know him?

Zac's younger brother Ben, of similar fortune and similar looks, cannot have failed to have noticed his brother's image transform from unfathomably rich toff to guru on all things environmental. He, too, saw Green was good and turned his back on the less environmental businesses upon which he'd cut his teeth (Quintessentially) in favour of things of a Greener hue.

A HOUND NAMED OTIS

Why not copy the heir to an earldom and an impressive chunk of England in the North? Still a teenager, he draped his inherited house in the Kings Road with banners urging Londoners to boycott supermarkets. After being ordered to take it down by the council, he went on to set up an online community of 'activists, academics and anyone who cares' to help save our green English world.

And what about the glamorous son of this country's richest banking family? Not content with merely being rich, he wanted to put something back too, and so set up a 'resource' enabling him to jet off to the North Pole with sixteen Inuit dogs and 35 kilos of chocolate in the name of the planet. Not only is he doing his bit – apart of course from clocking-up air mileage (he also divides his time between London and New York) – but in the name of finding out more about global warming he is planning several 'mini missions' to South America, Uzbekistan, the Pacific Ocean and China in 2008. He can go global with a clear conscience and a carbon offset.

The Green-Wash

If you're the child of the incredibly rich, or the famous, or the merely aristocratic, why spend your life being resented by the nation? Why not become revered overnight by getting a conscience and going Green?

Consider the son of the rock star who spent thirty-six hours in jail for infiltrating the House of Commons, grabbing the mace in the debating chamber and haranguing the rural affairs minister. From unknown son of a celebrity to Eco-hero overnight; hounds up and down the country have been named after him ever since.

Equally if you are the son of no one in particular, why not take a stand, go Green and get some positive publicity and some interest from this nation's top Eco Sloanes.

GREEN ISSUES

But there's a hidden danger in the Eco Sloane's world. The danger is that Green can bring the Eco Sloane closer to the unspeakable and the inedible. It can mean contact with the kind of Types of whom the Sloane is habitually nervous: the intellectuals, the left-wingers, the Marxists, those who advocate a complete sharing of resources – in short nutters who believe in wealth distribution. There are, after all, many shades of Green and the Eco Sloane prefers a paler, sanitized hue devoid of any threat of forcible dispossession and therefore any threat of politics. The Eco Sloane might have pondered this: the idea that he is a person with a lot of stuff, who is preaching to people with less stuff about the dangers (to the planet) of acquiring more stuff. However it's likely that he didn't. It's a tricky business and it's best not to think too hard about it.

SHOPPING

GROCER'S DUCHY

When Napoleon described the English as a 'nation of shopkeepers', he didn't mean it as a compliment. He was describing a petit bourgeois people more interested in buying and selling goods than in big conquests. One hundred and fifty years later, ever growing numbers of Eco Sloanes with four generations of soldiers behind them seem to think that shopkeeping is a rather more noble occupation than conquering foreign lands.

Eco Sloanes have followed the Prince of Wales' lead: they believe that grocers can

save the world. But there are shops and shops –
the Eco Sloane isn't planning to Tesco.
He knows that an eco grocery shows
a) that you have land, b) that you
can manage it, and c) that you
can produce a surplus which
can then be sold. You're
being enterprising and
entrepreneurial (what
better way to prove
you're posh). And
you're also setting a
fine example.

The first product in Prince
Charles' Duchy Originals range
was an organic biscuit made with oats grown on his estate. It took family baker
Walker's eighteen months and several biscuits to get it right for him (he's a man who
knows what he likes) and it finally went on sale in 1992. Despite the fact that it
earned the Prince the headline 'The Shop-Soiled Royal', and got eyebrows raised in
the hunting counties, Duchy Originals absolutely charged into the new millennium.
The company now has a selection of two hundred 'quintessentially British products'
which range from biscuits to bacon to shampoo and in 2006 Duchy Originals made a
profit – for the Prince's charities of course – of £1.2 million. It's Green, it's good and
it's highly aspirational.

Since 1992 other estates up and down the land have opened stores or gone online to
offer proof of what they're doing for the environment. We've got cheese from the
Cotswolds estate of a Britpop star and we've got rare breed sausages from the Dorset
estate of a marquess ('flagship' store in the local village and supplier to a range of
upmarket restaurants). These days we're offered meat, eggs, sausages and asparagus
from estates all over the land.

THE HARRODS OF THE COTSWOLDS – DAYLESFORD ORGANIC

The most successful farm shop in the land has been nicknamed 'the Harrods of the Cotswolds' by bemused locals.

This immaculate conglomerate of done-up barns and outhouses is a destination shopping centre, a kind of organic Bluewater for the richer day tripper and weekender. Established by the Bamford family which owes its fortune – and it is a fortune – to construction equipment sold globally, produce here is not cheap: 65p for a pint of milk and £2.25 for 400g of seven seed sourdough bread. The public can't get enough of it and the empire is expanding rapidly. There are already outlets in Sloane Square, Selfridges, Clifton Nurseries (Maida Vale) and Pimlico and of course the flagship store in the Cotswolds which has expanded beyond veg, biscuits and meat into clothing and new-age 'cashmeres for relaxing and gentle exercise; essential oils, candles and beautiful fragrances'. And now there are yoga classes. It's perfect: organic, new-agey and convenient for Blenheim and great chunks of Gloucestershire.

'We believe that preserving the environment goes hand in hand with better quality food,' is the claim of the Harrods of the Cotswolds on its website. It sounds ineffably right and it's certainly an interesting about-turn that something is being returned to the land by the family which built its environment-saving empire on the back of the profits of its land-razing one (JCB). Hurrah!

Daylesford Must-Buys

Six Cumberland sausages: £4.40
Ginger loaf cake: £5.75
Fruit-cutter with holster: £32
Suede apron: £125
Seasonal salad bag (for 4-6): £10

NOT CALLED 'GREEN-BACKS' FOR NOTHING!

Do you have to have inherited serious money to do Green in style? Despite the fact that being Green means spending four times as much by eschewing the supermarket for the Farmers' Market, the savvy Eco Sloane has worked out how to make Green work for her. Green can be a green light to making cash. And here's how: the Eco Sloane has realized that the world is waking up to Green and the fact is that money spent on Green goods goes some way to off-setting a carbon footprint or a mixed personal history. 'Organic', 'fair trade', 'environmentally sound' are just some of the key words the Green pound looks for. If your Green brand ticks these boxes, the eco shopper will have no qualms about spending two, three or sometimes four times as much on your product.

The demand for organic has seen Eco Sloanes move in on the organic deli and on the eco lunch market: 'Eat with your head'; 'The Real Food Company' and 'We're about making healthier, tastier food easier for you' are just some of the slogans from the eco end of the High Street – on the ethical clothing market as well as these faster-earning sources of eco cash. There are certain Eco Sloanes whose hunger for cash even the fastest expanding chain of eco food outlets can never satisfy. For them there is venture capital.

This in fact is how Ben sees himself. He co-founded his venture capital fund two years ago while still working full-time for the American investment bank. If he's entirely honest it was the

co-founder who had the idea and the know-how, but Ben is certain that it was his hunger which saw the whole thing through. After all, the size of his co-founder's trust fund is well documented. Credit where credit is due: it was his colleague who turned to Ben over dinner and told him that 'Kyoto is a huge opportunity,' and so their company was born. It has already raised several billion from global investors for the reforestation of the millions of deforested acres on this planet which are to be sold off to the Green-minded individual in carbon credits. Brilliant.

And then there are other schemes which started small and have since gone stratospheric. Take, for example, the humble organic veg box:

Abel & Cole started off as a potato and egg delivery service out of a basement in Catford. It went organic in 1993 and the company, which now has 25,000 customers, is expected to turn over £20 million in 2007. Any Eco Sloane worth his salt gets a weekly box and Tara looks forward to discovering what's in hers every Thursday. They're proud to have it sitting on their doorstep – often for most of the day: it's a badge which shows they're doing their bit. The one problem is that the contents are often an indecipherable mystery – Tara often spends fraught evenings struggling to get her head around fennel bulbs. Often she ends up having to throw them out, surreptitiously – brown and soft – a month later. She used to take them down, at weekends, to her mother's wormery but, what with Uma and everything else, it's just all too much to organize.

Other Eco Sloanes are less ambitious in their money-making ventures. They go in for more romantic, adventurous, low-impact outfits in the form of hand-sourced, fair trade slippers, nighties, freshwater pearls, sourced direct from the producer in Cambodia, India or Sri Lanka and brought home – in the hold – to be sold before Christmas. These Eco Sloane 'Tupperware parties' are a great way of helping third-world producers by flogging their goods directly to a sympathetic network of West London based friends. If all goes according to plan, Eco Sloane should make enough cash to fund another couple of trips back out to scout for more ecologically sound goods. It's a wonderful way for the Eco Sloane to justify at least six long-haul flights a year and a nice beachfront house preferably somewhere near where their grandfather was once Governor-General.

Some Eco Sloanes are content to operate at this cottage-industry level while others have opened fair trade shops in outer Chelsea (SW10) and other (more established) Sloane areas of London. The web is littered with their efforts, and 'beautiful yet sustainable products' are available through the post to any address: see, for example, The Lazy Environmentalist, and look out for goods including a ball of string ('80 metres of biodegradable spool of undyed jute twine') for £12.80; a candle ('biodegradable soy-wax candle handmade in the UK with a wick of 100 percent unbleached cotton') for £28. They might seem expensive but in terms of lightness of carbon footprint, this is certainly the green pound being well-spent: a thoughtful and generous present from one Eco Sloane to another and perhaps – for some, anyway – a slightly more satisfying gift than a goat for Africa, a bicycle for a midwife or ten yards of hedgerow. The Old Sloane impulse for completely useless presents never really died.

Eco Sloane's Problem Veg

kohlrabi • globe artichoke
chard • onion squash • celeriac alfalfa

GREEN DAY: FARMERS UNITE!

Green is a lifestyle choice. And if the mini-farm is already in place, there can be no higher ambition for the Eco Sloane than weekend farming. A few rare breed pigs (sausages are sold out the back); sheep; cows; a couple of acres of turnips; friends down from London and perhaps a regular column in a newspaper, 'The Trials and Tribulations of the Farmer'. It would provide a useful means of, say, bringing to the attention of the greater public the challenge of driving one's prize hogget after it's stopped being lamb and before it becomes mutton) up to town (ghastly traffic!) to sell to the chef at the Ivy.

Hobby farming, toy farming, hedge fund farming, weekend farming: there's nothing more satisfying than working the land. Marx knew it, Tolstoy knew it and the Eco Sloane knows it. It has little in common with any other kind of farming: say, for example, the tenant farmer who is bullied below the poverty line by the supermarkets, has to get up before sunrise and doesn't even have the value of his own land to fall back on. But Eco Sloanes do support every kind of farmer as the Liberty and Livelihood march showed. When not marching, this group will demonstrate solidarity by paying triple at their weekly Farmers' Market. Hard to know, however, whether the rare breeds sausages are a product of the 'hobby farmer' who also has a day job, or the struggling, salt-of-the-earth variety.

HUGH FEARNLEY-WHITTINGSTALL

St Hugh of River Cottage is the uber hobby farmer. He's an Eco Sloane superhero (despite frying off his friend's placenta and serving it on toast on TV). He is everything a Sloane loves: Old Etonian; Oxford; Gloucestershire (now Dorset) and he's living the dream. He says: 'Although I am now pretty much self-sufficient in pork, beef and lamb, I still like to top up my meat supply with flesh garnered from the wild.' This includes roadkill and other animals shot for the pot. These are important Sloane values: squeamishness in any form suggests louder than anything that an individual is not the real deal. In short there's nothing shiny about Hugh.

Even David Cameron, sensing that that was where Sloane affections lay, came out to announce how very much he admired Hugh for his 'contribution to the real food campaign'.

In 2004 Hugh, Jamie Oliver and Marco Pierre White helped Prince Charles to establish the Mutton Renaissance Club, a club supporting farmers who were struggling to sell off their older animals.

FARMERS' MARKETS

These are where the Eco Sloane shops. And London is braying with Sloanes picking up cheese or French sausages and organic cuts of meat: Sydney Street, Marylebone on a Sunday, Islington and Borough Market, in particular on a Thursday, to spend £25-plus on a leg of organic lamb and another £25 on a board of organic cheeses for a weekend dinner party. Some even take their London-bought country produce back to the country – from whence it came – for the weekend, in the back of the Range Rover.

BUILD IT

There are other ways of demonstrating one's Green credentials at home. But not all are suited to the average Eco Sloane: the Prince of Wales might wear a kaftan at home, but clothes are the least of it for the King of Green. He's building an eco house on the Welsh border now. It will have its own reservoir to collect and recycle rainwater, its own reed-bed sewage system, solar panels to heat the water in the summer, and a woodchip boiler for the winter. The house will be constructed from recycled brick and salvaged slate, the roof insulated with sheep's wool and the 60 cm thick walls will be padded with volcanic ash. And the whole will be inspired by the classical proportions of the Telesterion, built in 480 BC at Eleusis, north of Athens. It won't be completed until 2010 and although, once up and running, it is likely to save

significantly on bills, this eco house is not for the average Eco Sloane: its building is forecast to cost around £5 million (and that does not include the cost of the land which, in this case, was substantial enough for the reservoir… another £5 million).

The Eco Sloane applauds this on-going construction and yet, even if he did have the money, would definitely prefer to wait to see how the Prince gets on first: after all, we all need pioneers!

DRIVE IT

And so although the Eco Home might be an eco step too far, what's parked outside the house is just as important. Designed in California, built in India out of plastic, run entirely on electricity and shipped here on neutral carbon footing (transportation carbon footprint thoughtfully offset by the manufacturer) the G-Wiz has a top (downhill) speed of 40 mph. It needs charging every 30 miles – that is if you don't use the windscreen wipers, heating or radio – but still 850 of them, at between £6,000 and £9,000, had been sold in London by the summer of 2007.

G-Wiz lovers can't wait to tell you about their darling little car. 'I love my G-Wiz… such fun to drive, easy to park, nippy and it's great to be able to match anyone at a green light!' says Kristen Scott Thomas, London. Another delighted owner is Georgia Byng. Owners clubs have been set up and last summer they congregated for a picnic and general celebration in Regent's park.

These golf-cart like vehicles are frequently spotted on the Kings Road. Eco Sloanes at the greenest end of the scale drive these.

The Prince of Wales drives a hybrid Honda Prius.

JOIN A PARTY: A GREEN CAUSE IS A GOOD CAUSE

There's no denying it: green does wonders for your reputation. Consider Al Gore: from cerebrally challenged, forty-fifth vice president to star of Academy award-winning documentary, *An Inconvenient Truth*. Also Arnold Schwarzenegger: from body builder to Green governor of California whose commitment to the environment has almost brought on calls for his beatification.

In this country a Green-wash is equally effective. Consider David Cameron: install a wind turbine and solar panels on the roof of your house in Notting Hill (or even

merely promise to); host meetings in London's Wetlands Centre in Barnes; jet to the North Pole for a photo shoot with the melting ice caps; cycle to work; get several high profile Eco Sloanes onside as party advisers; and raise the profile to make your party sound altogether cooler and more party-ish.

Many an Eco Sloane enhanced their own reputation by marching with the Countryside Alliance. Ben summoned everyone in his internet address book, with rallying cries of 'For God's Sake Save the Countryside from the Commies', to Ladbroke Grove for free-range bacon sarnies and coffee before setting off on the two miles to Hyde Park and the start of the Liberty route of the march, wearing hunting coats and riding boots and clutching stuffed foxes. He was pleased to see that boys from his old school had been given the day off as had the pupils from Harrow and Cheltenham Ladies College (in return for the forfeit of one 'privy' – privilege). The ban went through but most hunts have since reported levels of support not seen since 'before the war' thanks to the efforts of the Eco Sloane.

Ben also does his bit by attending a drag hunt which was set up by an old school chum on April Fool's Day a couple of years ago. It came about when this friend was cautioned by a police officer in a London park for 'allowing' his dog to chase a squirrel. As this was after the ban on hunting with dogs, the policeman informed him that, by law, his dog could be put down, and he could be arrested and subject to a £5,000 fine. 'Absurd,' declared Ben's pal, 'the law is absurd and the best way of showing it is to obey it.'

GET SEVERAL HIGH PROFILE ECO SLOANES ONSIDE AS PARTY ADVISERS; AND RAISE THE PROFILE TO MAKE YOUR PARTY SOUND ALTOGETHER COOLER AND MORE PARTY-ISH.

THE COUNTRYSIDE ALLIANCE

The Countryside Alliance was formed in 1998 from the following pre-existing organizations: the British Field Sports Society, the Countryside Business Group and the Countryside Movement. The CA's head office is in Vauxhall, London, which is possibly the most urban spot – furthest from a single blade of grass – in the entire country.

Its formation was central to the Sloane revival for, over the past two decades, previous cornerstones of the Sloane system (the Church, the Tory Party, the Monarchy and the 'old' schools) had waned. In Blair's Britain there was little uniting the Sloane. In 1998, field sports – so beloved by the Old Sloane – were under threat, and so were farmers too. The Countryside Alliance formed a new banner under which Sloanes could unite and unite they did, in September 2002, when 400,000 farmers, ruralites and people who loved the countryside (Sloanes) descended on London to march in the name of Liberty and Livelihood.

The Countryside Alliance has been accused of having a single issue agenda – hunting
– packaged to include other issues, i.e. the plight of farmers, in order to garner
nationwide support.

Celebrities who marched: Vinnie Jones, Edward Fox, Diana Rigg, Nicholas Parsons,
Elle Macpherson, Clarissa Dickson-Wright, and former Conservative leader William
Hague were there. Even the white farmers of Zimbabwe pledged their support. The
Countryside Alliance 'I Was There' badge has become a medal and can be seen on the
lapels of Barbour and Schoffel jackets up and down the land.

The ban went through in February 2005. Incidentally, the plight of farmers hasn't
improved; even the Queen was forced to sell her dairy herd in May 2007 owing to
significant losses accrued over several years. The average price of milk is 19p a litre
while the average production cost is 22p a litre. What happened to the pint, asks the
Old Sloane.

THE CONNAUGHT SQUARE SQUIRREL HUNT

Named after the square in which Tony Blair bought his house, the
Connaught Square Squirrel Hunt was set up by joint masters Ed Seyfried
and Duncan Macpherson. It involves one hound (Seyfried's) and a sports
sock on a string. Livery is midnight blue velvet with pink collar and lining.
The hunt saw successful seasons in 2006 and 2007 during which
followers met on Sunday afternoons at the Duke of Kendal pub 'for port
or Pimms' before chasing the dog which chased the sock through
picnickers and tourists in Hyde Park.

Supporters include Rhys Ifans, Otis Ferry and Jeremy Irons and the
'annual ball' at the Banqueting House habitually makes several pages in
Tatler's Bystander section; revellers end up dancing the night away either
at Boujis or
Annabel's,
depending
on age.

HUNT

It's important to hunt – but not with just any old hunt. After all, it's less about the fox and more about the people. The anti-hunting bill united the Sloane and since the ban, every Sloane (even those born, bred and raised in London) has been called to the field; the waiting list for a coat is longer than it's been since the First World War.

There is hunting and then there is hunting. And hunting should be a grand day out.

- **The Heythrop** straddling Goucestershire and Oxfordshire.
- **The Quorn** Leicestershire.
- **Blackmore Vale** Dorset and Somerset.
- **Duke of Buccleuch's Hunt** Berwickshire, Roxburghshire.
- **The Belvoir** based at Belvoir Castle and home to the Duke of Rutland. The Prince of Wales and Viscount Linley have both hunted here.
- **The Beaufort, near Highgrove** it's a favourite with the Prince of Wales and the Duchess of Cornwall and also with Princes William and Harry.
- **South Shropshire** for the more celebrity-minded Sloane. MFH is Otis Ferry, son of Bryan, and he's managed to entice celebrities like Sienna Miller out for a day.

For the Sloane who is serious about hunting and who finds things just haven't cut it since the ban, there's always Ireland. Each of these is blessed with a smattering of Sloanes:

The Louth, The (Killing) Kildares, The Galway Blazers

SHOOTING

Shooting has never been more popular: 600,000 people are involved in shooting in this country now. There is an interesting tension between the Old Sloane, whose father shot and his father before him, and the New Gun. For the first time the Sloane is outnumbered on the field by the corporate sector, by Americans, bankers and plutocrats.

While the Sloane traditionally would have shot his first pheasant at nine or ten years old on his father's estate, that's not the way things work now; new money has bought up tracts of land previously owned by the Sloane.

There are, however, ways for the Sloane to stay in the game.

Unlike London, Old Sloane rules still apply out in the field: the scruffier the Gun the more likely he is to be grand. Shooting clothes should not be too shiny, too new, too expensive. Sharp Savile Row suits with leather trim smack of Americans. The smart Sloane wears a comfortable old jacket, Schoffel perhaps or Barbour (though not waxed) and uses a family gun – none of this over-and-under nonsense.

Of course in an ideal world the Sloane should never pay for a day's shooting, he would only ever be invited. The day would start with 'Bullshots' (consommé with vodka) some shooting and then a splendid lunch! Ah!

THE QUARRY

Grandest is grouse, then partridge and pheasant. But of course the main thing about shooting is where one does it; anything with Royal associations comes, perhaps unsurprisingly, top:

- Sandringham – the Queen
- Holkham Hall – the Leicester family
- Lauder – the Duke of Northumberland's 9,000 acre grouse moor in Scotland

BARBOUR

The waxed jacket is no longer the choice for Guns but the Barbour is back in demand thanks to Lord James Percy's involvement (the youngest brother of the Duke of Northumberland – best shot in the country – some would say). On meeting Dame Margaret Barbour (the chairman of Barbour) at his family estate in Linhope he declared: 'Dame Margaret, can I just say something about your coats? They're beautifully made and all that, but they're pretty crap for actually doing anything in. You can't swing a cat or shoot a pheasant in them.'

She was rather taken aback until the young man whipped out four prototype coats he'd been working on. In Lord James, Dame Margaret immediately recognized an expert: 'He's such an attractive-looking man, isn't he? I mean, what better representative could there be than him?' she said. Percy's first collection for Barbour came out in the autumn of 2005 and was made up of just four shooting jackets which featured the following improvements: sleeves which are engineered to allow the wearer to raise a gun; moleskin which is used because it doesn't make any noise; breathable, Teflon coatings rather than waxed cotton; and pockets that can be buttoned open while the wearer reaches for cartridges. Since then Lord James has added other items to his inaugural collection, including a leather gilet and a yard coat and once again the Barbour is favoured by the Sloane Gun.

"WOULD YOU LIKE ME TO HOLD YOUR COCK?"

Paraphanalia

No Country Sloane loo is complete without one of Bryn Parry's shooting cartoons – etiquette, common faux pas and Agas – particularly a slightly risqué one.

SAVE SLOANE SQUARE (SSS)

And then the opportunity to save Sloane Square came along. Concerned about traffic congestion, the council for the Royal Borough of Kensington and Chelsea proposed a £5 million scheme to create a new road through the middle of it, making two smaller pedestrian squares, one at each end.

The issue was raised in October 2005 in the House of Lords by the heroically voiced Baroness Trumpington: 'My Lords… I am particularly concerned with the future of much-loved Sloane Square [and] the local council's scheme to convert Sloane Square into a crossroad at the cost of at least £5 million.

In fact Sloane Square is a dark, paved area without sun, seating or a café. It is populated by pigeons, the occasional drunk and occasionally over-excited A level students on their summer holidays splashing about in the fountain with champagne. However its perceived threat proved a good cause under which Sloanes could unite.

And so the Save Sloane Square campaign was established. The list of patrons, several of whom live outside the borough, makes impressive reading, or as the SSS campaign explains, it's 'a *Who's Who* of distinguished patrons from all walks of life'. Names include Clive Aslet (former editor of *Country Life*), Rupert Everett (film star), Hon. Lady McAlpine (wife of Sir William), Dame Antoinette Sibley (ballerina), the Dowager Marchioness of Salisbury (garden designer), Lady Lancaster (a former editor of *Harpers & Queen*), the Marchioness of Worcester (environmental campaigner) and Pierre Spengler (film producer of *The Prince and the Pauper* and the *Superman* Trilogy). It is, in short, just the kind of campaign to which a Sloane should add their name.

The SSS came up with its own scheme to improve the area which centred upon the planting of box hedges. And the SSS was 'delighted' when the Royal Borough bowed to such luminous pressure and withdrew their plans. Another Sloane success!

THROW A PARTY

If Green politics is tainted by the shadow of Marxism, the Eco Sloane need not despair. If one is wary of joining a party, why not throw one instead? Green is socially smart and the key to getting close to leading Green lights is to hit on the right Green cause. The Eco Sloane keen on getting on will choose a cause for which he can host a party and attract some top interest. Will protesting against Tesco cut it? As Ben is well aware, some causes are going to be more about standing on kerbs on the outskirts of towns holding banners in all weathers than about getting the Prince of Wales to throw open his doors. The key is to pick a cause which could see you featured on a double page in *Tatler* standing next to the Prince of Wales and any number of the ubiquitous Green Rockocracy.

THE GREEN ROCKOCRACY

- Bob Geldof

- Bryan Ferry

- Sting and Trudie

- Bono

- Eric Clapton

WHAT TO WEAR

It's rubbish that Eco Sloanes can't be glamorous. Look at Eco Sloane icon Sienna Miller for example. Her favourite clothing label is People Tree, the ethical catalogue which specializes in ethical and low-impact fabrics and dyes. Does she look unglamorous? What about Anya Hindmarch's bag, the celebrated 'I'm Not A Plastic Bag'? Even if it hadn't been modelled by Keira Knightley and Lily Cole, the queue of women eager to get their hands on this coveted item (£5) could not have been mistaken for anything other than a line-up of London's most glamorous Eco-Vixen Sloanes. This bag was the height of glamour.

In fact, the canny Eco Sloane has seen that there's money to be made here: If Bono and his wife Ali Hewson can tap into this burgeoning market for stylish high-end ecologically responsible Sloane fashion with their clothing company Edun, then why can't the Sloane?

BEN'S GREEN PARTY

Ben was delighted to have been asked to Zac Goldsmith's £10,000 a ticket poker tournament at FIFTY in St James's last year. Held in aid of the Shane Warne Foundation (a children's charity) and the Ecology Trust, everyone was there: Sting, Trudie, Jemima, Hugh, Sotheby's chairman Henry Wyndham, Sir Philip Green, David Tang, Tom Parker Bowles. Yes, Zac might be well connected, however Ben's point is not a bad one: if the charity's right, who knows what support might come from which quarters?

And so Ben has started doing his bit and is getting a bit of a name for himself in West London as being fastest off the blocks when it comes to rapid response fund-raising for one natural disaster or another. Take the earthquake at Bam: the day after it happened Ben, who has a special interest in Iran (having spent a week there during his gap year when he travelled through central Asia) had secured an Iranian lutenist, booked a hall he knows just off Marylebone High Street and thrown open his internet address book. Six days later, on a Thursday night, having cancelled their plans for dinner and each paid £50 for the privilege, a legion of Eco Sloanes from West London arrived dressed in black with discreet jewellery. They listened to the lutenist, drank champagne and paid a further £10 per ticket for the tombola which was a brilliantly lucrative idea of Tara's (she'd organized donations from several well-known shops and off-licences in W11).

One week later Ben was able to send an extremely respectable cheque for £14,800 to the Earthquake Appeal.

In spite of there being standing room only, not as many chairs in the hall as Ben had anticipated, and the lutenist being difficult to hear, London's Eco Sloanes came in their droves to raise money for a disaster on the other side of the world that was definitely the result of carbon emissions and global warming. Alas, the Prince of Wales couldn't attend but the details of his charming decline provided great entertainment for guests during Ben's 'impromptu' speech. Various other well-known Eco Sloanes plus their wives did pitch up, along with a high ranking representative from the Iranian Embassy and thanks to the presence of one well-known Eco Sloane (who had been photographed the previous week in a compromising position with cocaine) the photographs made one national newspaper and the Londoner's Diary in the *Evening Standard*.

The lesson learned? Green brings the A-list, and these days the best A-list parties are Green.

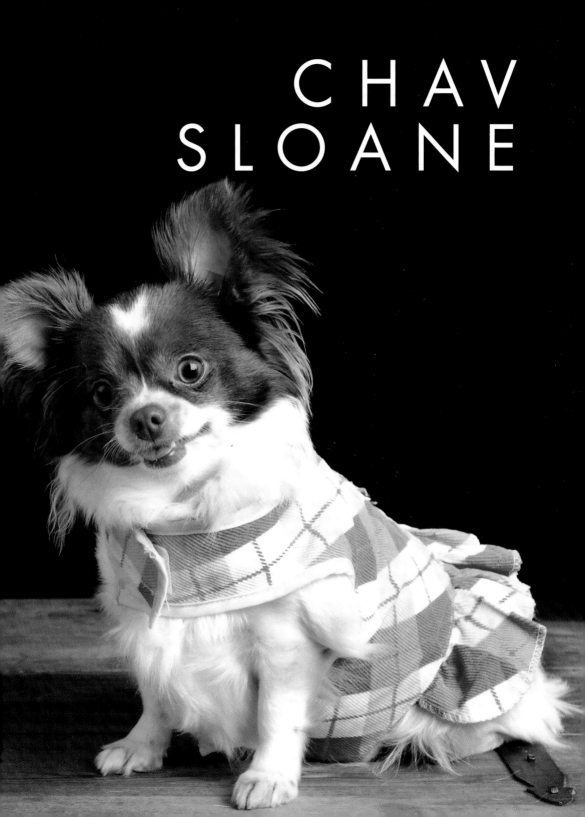

CHAV
SLOANE

THE TRAGIC CASE OF BURBERRY

Twenty-five years ago Burberry was a staple in every Sloane's wardrobe. A British outdoor clothing company founded in Hampshire in 1856 by enterprising 21-year-old Thomas Burberry, what could be better? Burberry was about utility and, for the Sloane, utility represents rightness. (Similarly Barbour: it's got such big pockets that you can stick cartridges in one and rabbits in the other; also Drizabone: the Aussie equivalent which took off when Barbour became too popular.)

Through the late 1980s and early 1990s, Burberry was made infinitely more recognizable by a new American CEO and a strong marketing push. It became recognizable as good quality, as 'old British'. And then it became fiendishly recognizable.

The Chav, like the Sloane, loves anything recognizable and so Burberry, with royal warrants from both Prince Charles and the Queen, became the greatest Chav brand of all time. The final nail in the coffin came when Daniella Westbrook and baby were photographed head-to-toe in the legendary beige check.

Burberry still features in the Sloane wardrobe but as something to be brought out for the (frequent) Chav fancy dress party.

THE CHAV SLOANE

The Chav Sloane comes in three varieties: the Chavtastic, or Chessex, type who is fully signed up to the cult of self – previously deeply un-Sloane: designer gear, fake tans, parties, celebrity. Then there's the Inverted Sloane, the one who works hard to disguise Sloane origins, speaks mockney and never mentions his background. This second type might have found that Sloane actively works against them in the workplace in New Labour's more plutocratic (chippy) Britain. Equally, the Inverted Sloane might be the kind who finds some areas of Chavdom – 'gangsta', say – deeply romantic.

And the third type, the Ironic Chav, is the one who is so confident of their Sloane status they freely use un-Sloane words such as 'toilet', 'serviette' and 'settee' without fear of anyone – anyone who matters, anyway – mistaking them for the genuine Chav article. They know the code which still matters to their country cousins and they just *love* breaking it. Like the song they want to 'do whatever Common People do'.

Meet

Bella (Bells)

Bella, 30, went to Benenden and then to Oxford (Brooks) where she read History of Art (2:1). She grew up in Hampshire but you'd never know it to look at her: with her year-round tan and white-blonde hair you'd be more likely to think Alderley Edge. She works as a PR for an Italian clothes designer (she describes herself as a 'brand ambassador') with several shops in London including the flagship on New Bond Street and one – conveniently for the flat – at Brompton Cross. She (semi) lives with her boyfriend, Chas, on the Kings Road and while the location is fabulous, the flat is minute. The main problem is her shoe collection: 124 pairs at the last count (Jimmy Choo, Christian Laboutin, Manolo Blahnik – many of them free from the designer) and at least ten pairs of pumps from French Sole – and all kept in their boxes with a Polaroid on the front so she always knows where she's at.

If it was only she who collected shoes, that would be – just about – alright. The trouble is, her boyfriend collects shoes too. He has

She's partied with Madge and Guy (before they had the kids), with Sadie and Jude (separately, of course!), with Sienna...

over fifty pairs of trainers including several sought-after, one-off designs and vintage numbers. And for some reason – perhaps because he spends most of his time round at her place because he shares his South Ken house (it's been in the family since it was built) with his various brothers, uncles, cousins and whoever else is in town – he chooses to keep them all in Bells' tiny one-bed. In spite of the storage issues, she loves her boyfriend, not least because he is a DJ favoured on the celebrity circuit; not only does he know Prince Harry, but his job also means that Bells and her friends are a fixture on the guest list to the VIP room at parties all over London. She's partied with Madge and Guy (before they had the kids), with Sadie and Jude (separately, of course!), with Sienna and anyone on the international circuit including Lindsay, Britney (once) and Paris who is actually really funny! Bells does her bit in Chelsea to correct the bad press which she feels Paris gets and springs eagerly to the heiress's defence at any perceived slight.

Chas has a title though you'd never know it to look at him, or indeed to listen to him. He drops his 'h's, says 'later' when it's time to leave and in fact speaks such good mockney that you'd be forgiven for assuming that he'd spent his childhood in the East End rather than in a seriously big house in Suffolk – which is open to the public. He went to Eton and then Newcastle where he read Theology and of course ran the university social scene.

Chas recently bought a white Porsche Carerra and a number plate off a friend: 'GR8 2 B ME'. Everyone knows the number plate and so it takes about two hours to get the one mile from the flat to Sloane Square as they have to stop every thirty yards or so to say hello. Bells looks great getting in and out of that car: Dior sunglasses (she lives in them!); deep tan (she's permanently sun-kissed: she has a spray-on once every two weeks). A woman comes to the flat and on every other visit gives Bells a facial, shapes her eyebrows and waxes every last bit of hair off her (apart of course from that on her head, which she takes off to be coloured by Josh at Real Hair). And, yes, she'll put her hands up; she has had Botox – twice.

She wears D&G, Joseph and some vintage. Currently she favours a white platinum and diamond necklace in the shape of a 'B' which Chas bought (and she chose).

Her prize possession – apart of course from her teacup Schnauzer, Elvis – is a photograph of herself coming out of Boujis holding onto Diddy (or is it Puffy? – anyway the artist formerly known as Puff Daddy) last June – wearing a fur coat (him not her!). He invited them on his yacht a couple of weeks later but twelve months on and she's still waiting for his call! A friend did get to stay a couple of nights aboard: apparently it was wild!

When she's not out (at least four nights a week) Bells loves spending time in her

Her prize possession – apart of course from her teacup Schnauzer, Elvis – is a photograph of herself coming out of Boujis holding onto Diddy.

Juicies in front of the TV on her BB Italia sofa sharing something healthy with Elvis – and if he's at home, Chas. Her favourite TV shows are: *Celebrity Love Island* (she knows several of the people who've appeared on it) and of course *EastEnders*. Her favourite food is Krispy Kreme doughnuts (regular glazed) – she limits herself to one a week. Her claim to fame – apart from her friendship with Diddy of course! – is the fact that Jack Nicholson made moves on her in Cuckoo last year.

More Chessex (Chelsea girls infused with Essex joie de vivre) than Chav, Bells rejoices in herself, knows how to pose to best advantage when being photographed and would like nothing more than for Chas to ask her to marry him. She had fantasized about getting married at Highclere Castle in Berkshire – her family have known the Carnarvons for years – until Jordan went and had *hers* there. Apparently that wedding has been the worst thing that ever happened to Highclere: bookings have plummeted!

The first time she took Chas down to meet her parents, you should have seen their faces! After lunch her father took her aside and said: 'Your mother's a bit worried. What does Chas actually do for a living?' Bells had laughed and assured them he wasn't a drug dealer. The revelation that he was rich and had a title seemed to do much to soothe their fears: her father emerged garlanded in smiles and offering invitations to this and that, even onto his boat.

Chas's real name is Constantine Charles, which Bells discovered in Ibiza last year when she saw his passport. She finds it wickedly funny – especially as he goes mad whenever she mentions it!

CHAVTASTIC

YOU, ME AND ONE

It used to be, back when the Sloane still lived in Chelsea, that 'me, me, me' was all very well for Americans, but it wasn't for the Sloane. The cult of self sounded rather common, rather pushy, rather fast and rather for people on the make. Sloane values were all about you, me and *one*. After all, would the Queen push herself forward?

Something extraordinary happened in 1986. Sloanes started going Chavtastic. In the wake of Big Bang, the City opened up, internationals moved in and the old school tie lost its currency. That year saw The Death of Gentlemanly Capitalism. London went meritocratic and the Sloane realized that meant that the best, the brightest, the sleekest and the sparkliest would win: it was worrying.

Come the early 1990s, the female Sloane was miles better educated, still well

connected but she and her parents were starting to realize that this wasn't enough to guarantee the prize – the big marriage, the serious money and the status.

And so the 'It-Girl' was born – or rather reborn. Writer William Donaldson observed that the term was coined in the 1920s to describe 'a young woman of noticeable sex appeal who occupied herself by shoe shopping and party-going'.

Occupation: socialite. It-Girls shopped and dressed and partied their way through the 1990s: famous for dresses, for freebies and in some cases for behavioural problems, It-Girls were famous for being – well – famous. This was a fame they maintained primarily by being photographed at parties.

Being an It-Girl became a profession when she started to command fees for opening her lovely house to magazines and for appearing on reality TV – as herself. She also became famous for her taste for celebrity boyfriends, harking back again to the 1920s and 1930s when countesses clamoured to go out with showbiz studs like Hutch and Paul Robeson.

THE ULTIMATE IT-GIRL

It was Diana, Princess of Wales, who was the first Sloane to take steps towards what is now recognised as Chavdom, to the pained bewilderment and outrage of Sloanes, except those – almost all then in their twenties – who thought they'd like a bit of what she was having. It was this princess – or Queen of our Hearts – who got down with the people. More important, Diana showed an entirely un-Sloane disregard for the old codes: she spent time at the altar of self. She spent hours at the gym; she went public with her bulimia, her unhappy marriage and the subsequent love affairs; she dressed to be photographed and courted publicity until she became a staple photograph in every magazine in the country – Diana front row at Fashion Week; Diana at the Serpentine Summer party; Diana in Versace, in Christian Lacroix, Ungaro and Chanel. She also surrounded herself with a coterie of New Age healers and celebrities often picked from the more flamboyant end of the spectrum: Gianni Versace, George Michael, Michael Barrymore and, of course, her beloved Elton. Diana had learned the value of being high profile; her new friends were no threat, they knew how to have a great time and they simply adored her.

Diana invited celebrities to the palace to meet the princes and she loved being photographed by the top fashion photographers, Mario Testino and Patrick Demarchalier. Very unlike our own dear Queen.

This was new territory for the Sloane who had previously subscribed to the idea that the grander a soul, the more likely she was to dress Down and Country and not care.

WHO'S WHO IN IT-LAND

TARA PALMER-TOMKINSON

Born in 1971, she grew up on an estate near Basingstoke, the daughter of a High Sheriff of Hants. She went to school at Sherborne and in 1995 her life as an It-Girl took off when she was photographed kissing Prince Charles at Klosters. Later the prince banned her from his ski parties after she allegedly flashed her breasts at Prince William. But TPT was already on her way. Inundated with freebies (Prada, Versace, Dolce & Gabbana, Ray-Ban, Mazda) she maintained interest through skimpy costumes, erratic behaviour, a public announcement of cocaine addiction, a stint in

I THINK I'M SUPPOSED TO BE GOING.

rehab and, finally, surgery to restructure her nose. Her other addiction was clear: her celebrity boyfriends have included restaurateur Mogens Tholstrup, pop star Nick Rhodes, *Full Monty* actor Hugo Speers and the Beatles' producer's son, Greg Martin.

By 2006 Tara had gone strictly A-list and that year she was linked with names including Pete Doherty, James Blunt and Robbie Williams. When told of the late Sir James Goldsmith's plans for a Referendum Party, the weirdly rather brilliant TPT allegedly replied, 'I think I'm supposed to be going.'

TAMARA BECKWITH

More plutocrat than Sloane, Tamara was born in 1970, the daughter of property tycoon and old Harrovian Peter Beckwith. She grew up in Wimbledon and went to Cheltenham Ladies College. Her school career was cut short when she left aged seventeen to have a baby, Anouska Poppy Pearl. She managed to combine motherhood with her career as an It-Girl and was soon an underdressed fixture on the party circuit. Exes include Sylvester Stallone, Charlie Sheen and Sharon Stone's brother, Michael, to whom she was briefly engaged. In 2005 she launched her own range of jewellery though nobody believes she wears it herself. As she explained in an interview: 'It's sold

DOES MONEY BUY YOU HAPPINESS? ... IT DOESN'T MEAN YOU WAKE UP EVERY DAY FEELING PERKY JUST BECAUSE YOU CAN GO SHOPPING.

on QVC; if you've already worn a £2 million necklace, costume jewellery worth £15.99 just isn't the same.' Despite this apparent lack of business acumen, she's wiser in other areas and when asked, 'Does money buy you happiness?' she responded sagely, 'It doesn't mean you wake up every day feeling perky just because you can go shopping.'

LADY VICTORIA HERVEY

Born in 1976, the eldest daughter of the 6th Marquess of Bristol and his third wife (his former secretary), and the half-sister of the legendary wastrel, the 7th Marquess John Hervey, Victoria left Benenden and after turning down a place at Bristol University, threw herself into modelling. She opened a boutique in Knightsbridge (customers included Victoria Beckham, Meg Mathews and Martine McCutcheon) which closed eighteen months later with substantial debts. In 2001 she was photographed at a party with her breast showing and began her It-Girl career.

She has been linked with restauranteur Mogens Tholstrup, businessman Seb Bishop, racing driver David Coulthard, rock star Mick Hucknell, designer Scott Henshall, former Boyzone member Shane Lynch, Nathan Roberts (winner of the television show *Model Behaviour*), and Freddy Windsor. 'I used to think my title would count against me in life, but I now realize it will be a great help,' said Lady V in 1996. Her younger sister Lady Isabella follows in her Gina clad footsteps.

I USED TO THINK MY TITLE WOULD COUNT AGAINST ME IN LIFE, BUT I NOW REALIZE IT WILL BE A GREAT HELP.

Chavtastic goes National Treasure
It-Girl TV credits

Tara *I'm a Celebrity Get Me Out of Here*, *Fame Academy*, *Celebrity Blind Date*, *Tabloid Tales*, *A Place in the Sun*, and *Cold Turkey*, in which she attempted to give up smoking with Sophie Anderton.

Tamara *I'm Famous and Frightened* and *So You Think You Can Teach?* Plus guest appearances on *Shooting Stars*, *Brass Eye*, *Loose Women*, *Celebrities Under Pressure*, *The Big Breakfast* and *Trigger Happy TV*. She was the first celebrity to be voted off *Dancing on Ice*.

Lady V *Celebrity Love Island*, *The Farm*. Co-presenter of *The Big Breakfast* and appeared in *The Priory*. She presented Channel 5's *St Tropez Summer* and *The Truth about Boarding Schools*.

Lady Isabella Hervey *Celebrity Love Island*, *Celebrity Masterchef*, Sky 1's *Vroom Vroom* and in 2004 she received a gold medal on Channel 4 reality TV show *The Games*.

REALITY TV

It wasn't long before the It-Girl found that a round of never-ending parties could be, (a) fraying on the nerves, and (b) seriously unlucrative. There was one logical haven for the Chavtastic It-Girl: TV.

It meant she could stay famous, be pampered and earn real money. The aim: to forge a new status as a – rich – national treasure along the lines of say, Trinny and Susannah.

TV came quickly to the same opinion: it's a rare show which doesn't believe it could benefit from a confident noisy Sloane not afraid to make a fool of herself (vital Sloane characteristic), willing to weep and curse and bare her soul for entertainment. Loved or hated, the It-Girl is always great for viewing figures.

But it's not every Sloane that's cut out for national treasure status: remember George Askew (Eton-educated great-grandson of the 4th Earl of Ellesmere), a contestant on *Big Brother 7* (2006). He walked out after thirteen days saying that fame was, and would be, too much for him. These values are in keeping with those of the trad Sloane: Bells' parents' values. Or even TPT's parents' values – remember them on *Comic Relief Does Fame Academy* (2007), mystified and excruciatingly uncomfortable as they clapped self-consciously beneath a mirrored disco ball while their daughter performed on stage below.

TRINNY AND SUSANNAH

The original Sloane national treasures, Trinny and Susannah have managed to turn themselves into national brands. How? On the face of things they could seem fairly hard going for average victims: all that 'Look at me I've got a broad arse' – when in fact they always look super-fabulous particularly standing besides a pair of plebby blobs.

Their Sloane credentials are faultless: Trinny went to Queen's Gate School in South Ken and her friends include Elizabeth Hurley and the Dent-Brocklehursts of Sudeley

Chavtastic photographs for the Sloane loo

- P Diddy
- Lindsey Lohan
- Paris Hilton
- Tinkerbell
- Prince Harry
- Kate Moss

Castle (see Turbo Sloane). Susannah, the daughter of an Old Etonian Guards officer, went to St Mary's Wantage in Oxfordshire, was hunting from childhood and had an eight-year relationship with Princess Margaret's son, Viscount Linley. Trinny and Susannah met in the early 1990s at a dinner party at David Linley's.

Trinny and Susannah may be found on unfashionable sofas near you but next time they're guiding a middle-aged woman in chewing gum grey pants through the lumpy minefield that is her bottom, imagine instead they're choosing a joint for Sunday lunch. Pleb or leg of lamb: spot the difference? But of course the Sloane hates a snob… (see Introduction and The Problem with Kate).

A CELEBRITY IS NOT FOR LIFE:
IT'S JUST FOR CHRISTMAS

Sloanes are interested in celebrities again. Between the wars, all ancient toffs were best friends with Noel Coward, with the Astaires (Fred and his sister Adele) and all the grand ladies knew Hutch and Paul Robeson. Louche aristos have always loved celebrities. And celebrities has often loved aristos.

However, in the same way that Sloanes got serious about the City post-1986, they saw a massive opportunity in celebrities: they were a means of getting ahead, a means of making money and a means of upping value. They had something to trade.

The Chavtastic Sloane adores a celebrity – if the celebrity's the right celebrity, it's a fabulous means of guaranteeing a page in one or other of the magazines – and they meet at parties and in various bars and clubs. The Sloane can be fickle though: being photographed with P Diddy or Kelly Osbourne coming out of Chinawhite might be fun for a couple of nights around Christmas, but next year? In Sloane-land a celebrity, if not hardore A-list, will be discarded, like a handbag, after one season. This provides a vital means of differentiation: a celebrity lasts a season, the Sloane is here for life.

TOFF-LOVING ROCK STARS INCLUDE

Jules Holland (married Christabel, the ex-wife of the Earl of Durham)

Bryan Ferry (married London socialite Lucy Helmore, Lucy is now married to Robin Birley)

Mick Jagger (his private life is very much 'Hello Jacob' [Rothschild])

FOR BETTER OR FOR WORSE

Sloanes can't rule out linking up for better or for worse with an entirely Chavtastic individual – or a celebrity. Think how marrying Madonna upgraded Guy Ritchie from Mockney Sloane to international A-list celebrity.

In the same vein, consider how Chavtastic Chelsey enhanced Prince Harry's reputation: from velveteen blue blood to royal red blood in one photograph. A shrewd choice of partner can prove you're oh-so-much more than just a Sloane.

Chavtastic Pets
Teacup sized: Yorkie, Chihuahua, Pug, Maltese, Pomeranian, Shih Tzu, Schnauzer

INVERTED SLOANE

No one wants to admit to being a Sloane these days, an early mainstream 1980s Sloane, that is. Why not? Because thanks to Harry Enfield, Lloyds, and the Conservative party, Sloanes are sometimes considered rather dim, outdated, unprofessional, drunk and even a little bit fascist. The Inverted Sloane will often go further than merely denying his provenance to escape that perceived stigma. This might also be fuelled by the very real (and not so real) feeling that in various professions, the Sloane is treated differently, with prejudice – is even persecuted – since the Old School tie and socks started to have less sway.

SLOANES UP THEIR GAME

In the new meritocratic Britain which has developed over the past twenty-five years the new requirement, above being posh, is to be capable. After Big Bang, London was inundated with foreigners: the arrival of ambitious, successful, cash-hungry Americans and Euros meant that the Sloane had to ramp up his game in all areas. City life was transformed: from leisurely starts and civilised lunches and long term loyalty to boot camp alarm calls, sandwiches at desks and short term commitment (and frequent firings, takeovers and closures). Tradition and stability died.

And so since the 1990s, the Sloane has toned down his 1980s style and has been systematically de-Sloaning himself in order to remodel and re-emerge along more American lines.

THE SLOANE WHO WORKS IN THE MEDIA

The media in particular is where the Sloane feels
he must disguise his background. Twenty-five
years ago Sloanes worked in media in so far as
the thoughtful, political and literary Sloane went
to the *Daily Telegraph* or *Spectator*. These days
however, things are different: a mass of Sloane
ambition focuses on media (journalism,
advertising, TV, film) and media-land at every
level is full of gently raised people dressing the part (down) and sounding the part
(Mockney). So London is full of Sloanes in disguise: rare is the real working class
person at the BBC and the *Guardian* is full of closet Wykhamists.

It's the opposite of the old Terry Thomas/Leslie Phillips self-invented toff syndrome.

The truth is: they might speak mockney and pay lip service to unSloane opinion, but
it takes more than that to shake off the inbuilt Sloane codes (see Introduction).

MOCKNEY

These days, de-Sloaning starts early: if you arrive at a London day school and sound
too flutey and posh, more worldly little boys might attack you. Children going from a
nice house in a provincial town to a nice boarding school somewhere in the
countryside are liable not to have to go Mockney so early. It's the rough and tumble
of the city that makes Mockney. It's all about survival, so Guy Ritchie doesn't want to
sound like a Fulham Road dilettante – in short, his parents don't sound like him. This
shows the collapse of the self confidence of the Sloane class: the previous generations
would have obliged their children to 'speak proper' or disown them until they did.

And so it is not uncommon for the corridors at some of this nation's finest schools to
echo with a lexicon garnered from a variety of places including 1950s boarding
school, gangster and Chav: the following are just some examples of words garnered
from the Chav side of the Sloane lexicon.

> **'Yo Blud! Exeat this kend?'**
> *Hello friend. Are you going home for the weekend?* **'Londres Innit!'**
> *Yes to London.*
>
> **'Same!'**
> *I am also in London for the weekend.* **'Safe! Let's hook up tomoz. Anyone for the KR?'**
> *Excellent let's meet tomorrow. Does the Kings Road suit?*
>
> **'Wicks!'**
> *Great idea.* **'Laters bruv!'**
> *Goodbye, friend.*
>
> **'Laters!'**
> *Goodbye.*

TOFFS AND TUFFS

For Sloanes romance blossomed in identifying oneself with rock stars and gangsters. It became appealing to somehow be like them, hence the almost gay strand in Mockneyism. There was the very real enjoyment of being around East End bruisers. Regency cartoons will show a celebrated pugilist, a working class gorilla surrounded by fantastically decadent toffs. The Krays' penetration of polite society is another example: a lot of fashionable people were drawn to the Krays and they became figures on the celebrity circuit. They were photographed – several times – by David Bailey and they associated with showbiz and aristos including politician Lord Boothby in particular, with whom it is said Ron had a relationship.

There is a revealling scene in Guy Ritchie's *Lock Stock and Two Smoking Barrels* (1998) when Vinnie Jones kills a group of effete public school drug dealers: Guy Ritchie kills off his own background in favour of the superior might of the gangster.

A HISTORY OF MOCKNEYISM

In 1968, Old Harrovian James Fox was cast as the gangster in *Performance*. This provided perhaps the first brilliant bit of Mockneyism: an almost classical young actor (he had previously been type-cast as the archetypal toff in *The Servant*) entered the louche world of gangsters. There was an edge to his performance which set a lot of well-brought-up boys thinking.

Even the story of how he trained for the part resonated: Fox spent time at the Thomas à Beckett, a one-time boxers' pub and gymnasium on the Old Kent Road, where he mixed with people like Johnny Shannon, the notorious boxing trainer, and John Bindon, a local hard man who'd slept with Christine Keeler and was celebrated for his ability to balance six half-pint beer mugs on his penis. By the time Fox came on set, this gentle public school boy had learned to hit, had gone out on a dry run for a robbery and spoke seamless public school mockney.

Prior to *Performance*, it was unheard of to speak mockney. At that time, (thanks to the Beatles), the fashion-conscious Sloane was still trying his luck with the Liverpudlian accent and northern expressions such as 'gear!' and 'grotty'. See, for example, the late John Peel aka John Robert Parker Ravenscroft, educated Shrewsbury.

IRONIC CHAV

He might wear white suits. She might wear white stilettos. She might wear an anklet and he might have a personalized number plate and a heavy gold bracelet at his wrist. He might look vulgar and extrovert but he's not vulgar and extrovert in the same way that Wayne Rooney is. He does it with panache. In short, he dwells at the grander end of Sloane in a world which sparkles and glitters with the elevation of downmarket items. Think, for example, of the Queen's loyalty to *EastEnders* (including, it is said, the Sunday omnibus).

Wayne Rooney charters a jet to take fifty of his favourite people for a long weekend to Barbados: that's naff. The Ironic Chav Sloane does it and suddenly vulgar displays of wealth become cause for lavish celebration: it's just great to be so fabulously rich.

Consider the daughter of a celebrated peer whose family is famous for extravagant parties. Her mother is the host of the year whose guest list runs all the way from the Prince of Wales and the Duchess of Cornwall to hot actors and the odd celebrity rapper. She chooses to holiday in Center Parcs. She is above having to try and *certainly* above having to subscribe to the code. She goes to Center Parcs because it's ironic and because it's 'relaxing' and 'everything you could possibly want is there'. Having to choose between Suffolk, Sherwood Forest, the Lake District and Longleat, she usually opts for Longleat as it's not too far from her parents' estate.

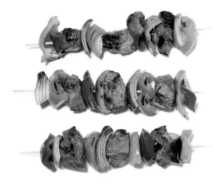

The Ironic Chav has no fear of shriekingly non-U words which, a generation ago, would have finished them socially:

- Toilet
- Lounge
- Settee
- Serviette
- Garage (ga-ridge)
- Kebab

If you're self evidently cool, confident and rich you just don't care: everyone knows who you are.

DAN MACMILLAN

With his gold tooth, trainer collection and 'gangsta' clothing range which he sells all over the world (Zoltar the Magnificant – the designs are obsessed with sex and death), you'd think Dan Macmillan had some kind of a gripe against society.

In fact he's the great grandson of Tory prime minister Harold Macmillan, heir to the title Earl of Stockton and has already inherited some £30 million of a rumoured £300 million coming to him from the family publishing firm.

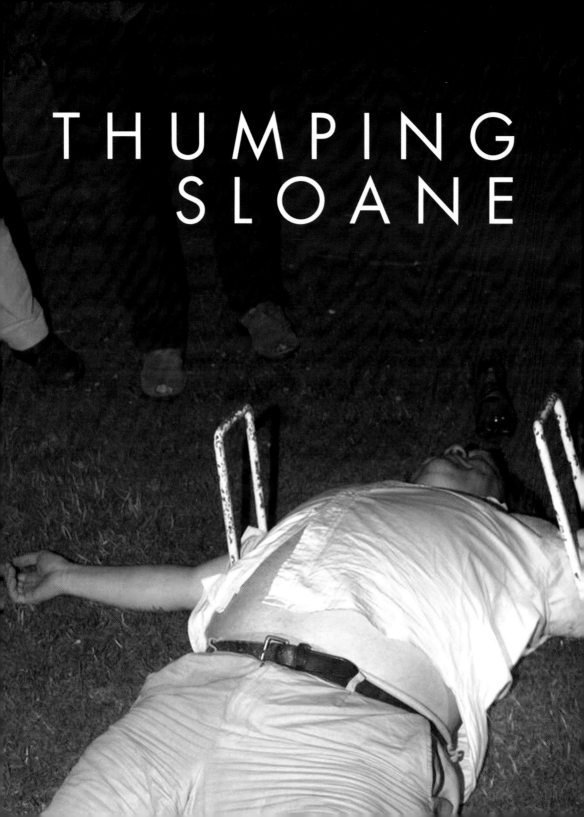

THUMPING SLOANE

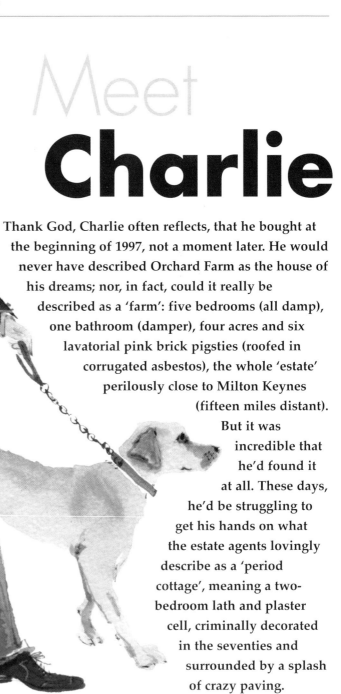

Meet

Charlie

Thank God, Charlie often reflects, that he bought at the beginning of 1997, not a moment later. He would never have described Orchard Farm as the house of his dreams; nor, in fact, could it really be described as a 'farm': five bedrooms (all damp), one bathroom (damper), four acres and six lavatorial pink brick pigsties (roofed in corrugated asbestos), the whole 'estate' perilously close to Milton Keynes (fifteen miles distant). But it was incredible that he'd found it at all. These days, he'd be struggling to get his hands on what the estate agents lovingly describe as a 'period cottage', meaning a two-bedroom lath and plaster cell, criminally decorated in the seventies and surrounded by a splash of crazy paving.

'Just camping at the moment,' he would tell friends who rang to see how he was getting on after he first moved in. It had been pretty squalid to begin with, though not as bad as that appalling year in the flat – if you could call it a flat – in Chelsea Cloisters, just after everything had gone tits up with Antonia (see Bongo Sloane).

Even now, eleven years on, Charlie doesn't enjoy looking back at his marriage. Blames himself. Ought never to have married her. They were chums, families had known each other forever, everyone said they suited each other so well, he'd quite fancied her. And, of course, he'd 'done the right thing' in the circumstances. (The shotgun 'guard of honour' – Ferret's idea, of course – had almost pole-axed his mother-in-law. Pity it hadn't.) He'd been twenty-five and Antonia a fortnight away from her twenty-second birthday. George had emerged six and a half months later, which was why (along with the later arrival of Louisa, of course) it had been worth doing 'the right thing', even though it had meant buggering up the next two and a half decades.

If Charlie was going to pinpoint the moment he knew it was going wrong, he'd say that it was when he'd moved to Fulham. He'd never liked Fulham, had just gone there because everyone else seemed to be: following the herd. But he'd always longed for the mews – backing onto Eaton Square (what had been the rent when he, Ferret and Bill first moved in? £10 a week for three of them?), an easy stride to the Antelope (who on earth goes there any more, Charlie wonders).

A bit of excitement, a bit of danger, that was what Charlie liked, which partly explained the extra-curricular developments once they were crammed into Rostrevor Road. Once, he'd seen Aspinall walking a tiger cub around Eaton Square and had said hello; didn't know Aspinall properly but had been to the Clermont a handful of times. And he was at the Antelope the night Lucan did his thing.

It was all routine by then: District line to Monument, brisk four-minute walk to the office. Charlie Gunton, stockbroker on the private client side. Not unduly demanding, it had to be said, certainly not as Charlie interpreted it ('Sell in May and go away').

That was about it. Generally guessed right more times than wrong. Had some very decent clients, too. The OEs patronized him, of course, once they'd learnt he'd been at Harrow.

The great thing about the City then was that it didn't interfere too much with Life, by which he didn't so much mean a few sets of tennis at the Hurlingham or Queen's, but the times when he broke free from London. Skiing was good, so was the Cresta. 'One day, you'll break your neck, darling,' Antonia used to say, ad nauseam, although by the end that was probably what she prayed for. But Charlie only really came fully alive when he had a gun or rod or rifle in his hand. Nothing better than Ferret's lodge in Sutherland. Oddly, Charlie never minded if he got a shot in or not. He just needed the physical challenge, the chance to haul himself across that landscape. Something sort of spiritual about it.

Couldn't get that in London, but he and Ferret used to jazz things up when they could. Captured a fox in Ladbroke Grove, put it in the back of Ferret's Bentley, drove it down to the VWH meet, and released it when everyone was knocking back the stirrup cup. The bloody thing ran straight into the pub car park! Didn't last long in there, of course – the hounds dealt with it in about seven seconds – but Ferret got it all on camera!

Charlie had been in the saddle as a boy – had to, with father and big brother in the 17th/21st – but he'd never really fancied horses. Except on a plate, of course. He'd had horsemeat in Morocco, probably in France too, come to think of it, not that the French ever let on. That's what Charlie rather admired about the French: did their own thing and sod everybody else.

But Charlie only really came fully alive when he had a gun or rod or rifle in his hand. Nothing better than Ferret's lodge in Sutherland.

Charlie wishes that Antonia had been like that. They'd watched Patrick and Arabella move to France (outside Carcassonne), and James and Potty open a B & B in Andalucia. Charlie had been tempted, not by France or Spain, but by Africa; more particularly by 'British East' as he liked to call it, where he'd stayed with Uncle Peter (who had a place on the coast, just out of Malindi) after he'd left Harrow. Peter was always on at him to come out and take over. Charlie had tried it on Antonia. 'I'll do the boat bit, take people out and get them catching marlin, you run the place as a guest house.' Seemed like a fair division of labour, but Antonia wasn't playing ball.

Then came the Lloyd's crisis. Something quiet, nothing bold, just a steady return was all he'd requested of the members' agent at lunch in Boodle's (they were both members, which Charlie had found encouraging). At first, it did what it said on the tin, and paid George's fees at Harrow – a helluva relief at the time. But the whole thing began to unravel at the end of the eighties – to the tune of £250,000. That

might not sound much to the weirdos and creeps in the City now, reflects Charlie, but at the time it represented the sum total of the Gunton fortune.

The whole thing had been gruesome, but he'd known he was on the way to recovery when he laughed at that letter in the Telegraph about whether or not The Archers was an accurate portrayal of country life. 'Of course it is not,' explained the letter-writer. 'There has never been a single mention of Lloyd's.'

By then, the divorce had gone through and Charlie was at Orchard Farm. Criminally biased against men though the system was, Antonia had been good in the end, as Charlie is now prepared to concede. Hadn't taken him to the cleaners in the way that she might have done.

George, stationed in Germany with the Queen's Royal Lancers (that absurd amalgamation that had swallowed up the 17th /21st), was making a bit by importing Audis; said he'd get one for Charlie, but Charlie had said no, he'd stick with the Toyota and hang onto his cash for the moment. Truth was, he hadn't got any cash to speak of. For the first five years at Orchard Farm, he alternated between commuting ('absolute hell') and grabbing a week at a time in Ferret's spare room in Chelsea. Food, oddly, was not a problem. He'd always been good at accelerating into rabbits (six in half an hour was his record – in Dorset, driving the Volvo). But these days he finds he does almost as well with pheasants ('astonishing the number of birds these Arabs put down'). And he times his run to the Tesco in Bicester just right (ten minutes before the meat in the chill counter gets marked down). Put enough Lea & Perrins on it and you're fine, says Charlie, who finds that Mr Tesco is also his wine merchant these days.

The reality was that he was still 'camping' seven years after moving in. That was when he bumped into Susie. Little short of a miracle, really. By then, he'd knocked the City on the head (if truth be told, it was the other way round, but the pay-off sweetened the blow) and had been so desperate that he'd been thinking about – no, more than thinking about: seriously considering – taking the plunge and trying that agency everyone always talked about, Amanda Duff-Creighton Introductions or something. Only the fee put him off. On the other hand, yet another evening of bridge at the Bearded Woman might well have driven him into it.

Food, oddly, was not a problem. He'd always been good at accelerating into rabbits.

But then Ferret had called him to London, said he'd treat him to dinner at Foxtrot. The timing was perfect: Charlie had just collected his chalk-stripe (and the herringbone) from Sketchley (first time in a year he'd bothered to get them cleaned: he'd been lured in by the two-for-one offer), so he thrashed the Toyota up the M40. He'd been well into his steak tartare and a bottle of CNDP, hearing what was what from Ferret, when who had he heard asking for Eggs Benedict but Susie? Turned out that Bill had ditched her for a forty-year-old Fräulein, leaving her to run the place in Perthshire on her own (with twelve bedrooms and a mile-long drive, it's a difficult one to pigeon-hole in the B & B guides). For which Charlie's damned glad. Always had a soft spot for the girl, but never quite closed the deal.

So now he's spending quite a bit of time north of the border, though they both know that that could change if the Jocks go completely Commie. But even so, all would not be lost: Uncle Peter's just cashed in his chips, leaving Charlie the place in Malindi. It's dodgy out there, but, at sixty-one Charlie's in the mood for catching up. So's Susie. What else? Well, it looks as though there might be a couple of quid from Lloyd's! All thanks to that billionaire called Buffet.

This, Charlie ruefully supposes, is what Antonia must have meant when she went on about 'the journey'.

THUMPER VALUES

Thumpers worship the F***ing Fulfords (that Channel 4 documentary about them was 'the only thing worth watching on telly for years'). Thumpers wish that they, too, could venerate twenty-three generations of ancestors, but make do with the five they've traced. They do at least know who their best friends are – friends made at home and school, in the army, and at Cirencester or more rustic agricultural colleges. Old Thumper sees London as an increasingly foreign country (Young Thumper thinks it much worse). 'Everywhere decent's closing.' Monkey's has gone; and what'll happen to Foxtrot, now it's in the hands of that bloody little Scottish footballer? Thumper struggles to find the sub for Brooks's, Boodle's or the Turf. He buys Boden, but only during the summer sale, which is when the second Mrs Thumper proves her worth, by making Thumper think about cords in July.

Thumper realizes, with astonishment, that it's now possible for Young Thumpers to fail the Common Entrance not only for Eton but even for Harrow, which had been full of King's Lynn thickos in old Thumpers day – he'd been one of them!

Thumper loathes Rock and Polzeath. 'They turn up dressed in Hackett, with God knows how much kit, as though they're about to go sailing, although they've never been in a boat in their lives, and dump their children. Unbelievably selfish.' Thumper reads The Field.

THUMPER RULES

- Eat curry and road kill
- 'Best-before' dates are for queers
- Death is part of life
- Accidents happen
- All the same, never point your gun at anyone (trespassers and burglars excepted)
- Give drink a chance

THUMPER ABROAD

Thumper's instinct tends to the traditional ('abroad's all right, except for the foreigners'), favouring anywhere which was once ruled by men in long khaki shorts. But, increasingly, he sees the virtue of moving to Spain or France.

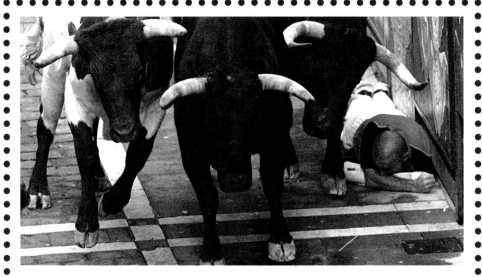

GOOD WAYS TO DIE, ACCORDING TO THUMPER

- Head first
- For Queen and Country (never for the Government)
- Having killed and (ideally) mutilated the burglar(s)
- On the bull run at Pamplona
- Meeting an impenetrable flock of sheep or herd of cattle at speed, preferably with impaired brakes, on the blind corner of a lane in Sloaneshire
- Making a sacrificial gesture

BOGUS ACHIEVEMENTS, ACCORDING TO THUMPER

Becoming a multi-millionaire by working eighteen hours a day in the City. Returning annually to St Moritz to do the Cresta Run. Do it once, says Thumper, or do it occasionally; never talk about it, never go to the Cresta Ball in London.

Running the marathon and talking about it, particularly talking about how much sponsorship money one's raised. If Thumper runs a marathon, he does so for a bet, in private, over Welsh mountains, very possibly with his entire inheritance at stake.

YOUNG THUMPER

GOES TO STOWE OR MILTON ABBEY

Has eaten squirrel, hedgehog and (for a £100 bet) rat (cooked rather than raw).
Never comes to London – associating it with Enemy Forces: Foreigners, and New,
Smug Money – a steadfast rule which he has broken only once in recent years, for
the Liberty and Livelihood March. Passengers waiting at Liverpool Street, Euston and
Paddington were appalled when the trains pulled in and battalions of Thumpers
spilled onto the platforms – red-faced, braying, intimidatingly flatulent.
Young Thumper travelled to Australia and Africa, been a tree surgeon, worked on a
farm, and now has two lorries and a van for moving furniture around Sloaneshire
(occasional breakages). He disguises his contempt for his customers – newcomers to
Sloaneshire – being all too aware of his financial dependence on them. Marriages, as
he and every other Thumper knows, almost always end in tears. Much better if you
love a girl. May have to wait. Perhaps till you're sixty.

THE TRAGEDY OF HACKETT

Thumpers young and old loved Hackett when it opened on the New Kings Road at the beginning of 1984, selling proper second-hand stuff – tweeds, serious suits, morning coats. Clever Jeremy H. Then it all seemed to go wrong, like the City. Today it's a brand, nice enough things, but worn by football hooligans and overpaid creeps and is no longer completely dedicated to Thumper's kind of Sloane.

THUMPER'S GUIDE TO THE ARMED FORCES

The Armed Forces offer Thumper a chance for a Proper Career, but some branches are patently more suitable than others:

- The Household Cavalry (the Life Guards and the Blues and Royals). The donkey-wallopers, Thumper calls them. An odd breed, the Life Guards especially – a mixture of shits (Ginge Hewitt) and spivs and terribly nice men. Down to two squadrons each.

- The Foot Guards (Grenadiers, Coldstream, Scots, Irish and Welsh). A mixture of Thumpers and Turbos (Charlie Mayfield: Radley, Scots Guards, chief executive of the John Lewis Partnership at forty).

- The Rifles (especially the bit that used to be the Royal Green Jackets). Again, a Thumper/Turbo mix.

- Elements within the cavalry. Thumper watches out for frauds (signet rings engraved with initials) and favours the 1st The Queen's Dragoon Guards (which hasn't been amalgamated).

- The Navy. Only really worth it if you want to fly helicopters, but if so, why not join the Army Air Corps? Thumper noticed the rest of the Navy when they arsed it up in Iraqi waters and ended up in Tehran, looking like extras from the staff room in Casualty.

- RAF. Don't be absurd

CLEVER THUMPER AND 'CAPTAIN' KIRKE

Occasionally, a Thumper with Brains is born, a genetic accident the consequences of which tend to find fullest expression at one of the ancient universities. Once there, Clever Thumper throws fridges from second-floor windows, drives golf balls at eighteenth-century glass, fires croquet balls at the heads of undergraduates slumbering in secluded gardens, climbs chapel roofs, impales himself on railings and experiences occasional nights in police custody.

After graduation (or other termination of his time at university), remarkable change is possible in Clever Thumper, who may mutate into Clever Turbo. Arguably the leading example of this is Richard Brindle, who, by the age of thirty-six, had accumulated a sum which friends estimated at £25 million, and who today is CEO of Lancashire Holdings Limited, a $1 billion Bermuda-based insurance organization which he founded in 2005. But once he was pure Thumper, boasting two convictions for drink-driving, and a 'double Third' in Greats, the latter achievement allowing him to become

a founder member of the Third XI, an Oxford cricket team composed of those with third-class degrees. The club colours were unashamedly nostalgic: 'Grey for the colour of the pavement on which we lay our heads, pink for the colour of our eyes, and blue for the colour of the light flashing in our rear-view mirrors.'

THUMPER SALUTES A HERO

About once a century, a Clever Thumper becomes a legend in his own precarious lifetime. Such a feat was accomplished by David 'Captain' Kirke (Wellington and Corpus Christi, Oxford), co-founder of the Dangerous Sports Club, who, in 1979, threw himself 250 feet off Clifton Suspension Bridge, thereby completing the world's first ever bungee jump. Since then, 'Captain' Kirke has hosted a black tie party on Rockall ('it took us five days to get there,' he remembered, 'and to leave we had to hurl ourselves off this rock in our dinner jackets; we were so drunk, we set off 180 degrees in the wrong direction towards Newfoundland'); skied down black runs attached to a grand piano; and had his spine rebuilt (with pieces of his hip) after a not entirely successful 600-foot base jump, off Ireland's Cliffs of Moher. He celebrated his 55th birthday by being fired from a 'human trebuchet' (a variation on a medieval siege gun), capable of hurtling a grown man 100 feet through the air.

The New Zealander who commercialized bungee jumping made a fortune. The Captain does not mind. Like any true Thumper, he knows that there is more, much more to life, than the accumulation of money. He and two others founded the Dangerous Sports Club, he has explained, because they needed to stretch the boundaries of human endeavour. 'We were doing all the commercial sports like the Cresta Run when we decided this had all been done by German industrialists to impress their mistresses… Remember that, for the English, sport is a distracted form of warfare.'

One of his co-founders has bought sixty acres near Bristol, earmarking the field as a cemetery for members of the Dangerous Sports Club, a spot that will be 'forever England'.

SLEEK &
EURO
SLOANE

Meet
Rose

Rose is a yoga instructor, a model and a painter but her first love – apart of course from looking fabulous, which is actually more of an occupation – is hunting. She's passionate about hunting, always has been. Her seventy-one-year-old mother still hunts, her grandmother hunted (granny rode – side-saddler, fearless and nearly blind – till she was eighty-five) and her great-grandmother hunted. When they're in the country, both Rose and her mother go out with the South Dorset.

Rose is forty-six. When was the last time she told anyone her real age? Longer ago than she cares to remember. People think she's thirty-four which is her intention, particularly with her modelling career in mind. She still does the odd designer travel show but these days makes most of her money from catalogues: she keeps quiet about those jobs!

As a yoga instructor, Rose specializes in one-on-one tuition in people's houses and also takes a couple of classes a week at a

The yoga is not about making money; even without the modelling assignments, Rose wouldn't need money thanks to the good whack she gets each month from her ex-husband, an American whom she left on Wall Street.

specialist centre in Notting Hill. She teaches yoga firstly because it makes exercising more fun and secondly because she's never been big on discipline: if she has a class to teach she can (usually) be counted on to show up.

The yoga is not about making money; even without the modelling assignments, Rose wouldn't need money thanks to the good whack she gets each month from her ex-husband, an American whom she left on Wall Street. He's rich and generous and pays very good maintenance for her and their thirteen-year-old daughter Poppy, who has recently started boarding at Heathfield St Mary's (formerly St Mary's Wantage, Rose's own school).

Rose began taking an interest in 'grooming' (she can't bear that word – it makes her feel like a horse!) when she moved to New York in the mid-1990s. She was in her early thirties then, beautiful and famous for being the muse of a French couturier. Her trademark look was Anglo-sloppy: she specialized in vintage jeans, scuffed boots and trainers with the backs trodden down.

Her nails were munched to the quick and sometimes she went for two days without washing her hair. Hers was the 'just-got-out-of-bed' look. Back in the UK she was considered breathtakingly sexy, but in New York this was not so: there she was veiwed with some concern: was she dirty, poor or depressed? Perhaps all three. Once when she arrived at a famous downtown restaurant wearing vintage Levis and a Biba top, the maître d' looked her up and down and then turned her away. Rose was horrified – she'd even booked a table.

For almost a year after that she hated New York. And then suddenly she succumbed. She'd started getting spots on her chin – a trauma she'd never previously suffered – so on the advice of her (one) friend in the city, she booked in to see a dermatologist. He suggested that she consult a nutritionist. The nutritionist advised her to follow a macrobiotic diet and visit a facialist. Rose booked in, liked the results, and the rest was easy: she lost a stone, got her hair straightened, took up yoga, had her eyebrows waxed and then endured her first Brazilian – despite the towel between her teeth, her howls could still be heard three blocks away. Back in London for Christmas, Rose spent a blissful two weeks with absolutely everyone gushing about how fabulous she looked.

As soon as Poppy was born, Rose treated herself to a post-partum boob job (though this of course is a secret between her and her surgeon) and her lifelong relationship with Sleek was confirmed. Her modelling work picked up and less than a year after Poppy's birth, Rose found herself on New York's Best Dressed lists; her signature look was 'classic chic'.

Back in London for good, Rose spent her first year putting together the coterie – all friends now! – whose task it is to keep her looking flawless. And she revels in looking flawless. Just the other day she wore a simple Prada column dress to the Ivy. Everyone else was in jeans and Rose stood out a million miles; every eye in that room was on her, and why not? It felt great!

Rose is generous when it comes to handing out names and numbers to her girlfriends – except of course for the special numbers that she keeps to herself. Her

As soon as Poppy was born, Rose treated herself to a post-partum boob job (though this of course is a secret between her and her surgeon) and her lifelong relationship with Sleek was confirmed.

colonic irrigationist, for example: there's something so, well, personal about the state of one's colon. And the woman who does her chemical peels – there's no need to tell everyone absolutely everything.

She must have given the number of her favourite person – Josh at Real Hair – to about fifteen people. All her closest girlfriends go to him. Not only is he utterly darling, he's also by far the best colourist in London and of course her warm honey tresses owe everything to him. She's under no illusion that she's his favourite person. Josh's favourite people are blonde, from Elle Macpherson through Laura Bailey, Jemima Khan and all the Anstruther-Gough-Calthorpes.

Rose feels privileged to be included on the legendary facialist Vaishaly Patel's client list. So exclusive is Vaishaly that Rose had to be recommended by an existing client, and the clinic's sign is so discreet that the first time she went there it took her ten minutes to find it. Vaishaly is also the best eyebrow threader in London, apart from, of course, the inspired and adorable Feroza at ColourNation in Covent Garden. As Rose tells her girlfriends: 'Never underestimate the power of well-shaped brows.'

If there's an important occasion like a wedding or a party at which she might meet her ex-husband and his new wife, first port of call is Fere Parangi and her little glass cubicle at Neville's on Pont Street. There's nothing so magical or youth-affirming as one of Fere's oxygen facials.

As for her other secrets, Rose is used to trotting these out at the request of beauty columns in various mags all over the world. She uses Dr Sebagh's Crème Vital, swears by Crème de la Mer's serum for puffy eyes, loves Eve Lom's cleanser, and could not live without her YSL Touche Éclat!

When it comes to pubic hair, Rose subscribes to the New York view that less is more and none is most. For these matters she goes of course to the celebrated Kamini Vaghela in Kensington Court.

Her nails are by Sophie at The Berkeley, her beautiful and perfect feet by Robin Oakey at Footopia. Her lineless brow by
Dr Sebagh himself. And as for any other queries? The answer is Of Course Not.

Of course I haven't had a brow
lift/boobjob/lipo/collagen/fillers.
Except of course Botox… Does that count? –
I wouldn't rule anything out. For some
reason the thought of everyone knowing
about the boob job is more than Rose
could bear. Instead she spends time
wondering who else amongst her friends
is similarly economical with the truth.

Rose has never felt better. She looks
amazing for her age and every man in
London is after her. Her mother on the
other hand thinks she spends too much
time and money on her appearance and
wants her to settle down in Dorset with a
nice man and give Poppy a stable home.
The last time Rose was down there her
mother suggested the recently widowed
Master of the Hunt, whom Rose has known
all her life (he must be sixty at least). She
is perfectly content to spend a season
following him, however she'd draw the
line at anything closer. She loves the fact
that the hunt meet swells to double if
she's going out, but she knows she could
never live down there full time: who would
shape her eyebrows?

SERVICE CHARGES

Gym membership in London might cost £100 a month. Then there are the monthly waxing bills of £100. Two facials at £120. Highlights at £100. Haircut £100. £20 eyebrow threading. £60 on manicures and pedicures. £200 on Pilates. £100 on Botox.

That's close to a grand each month before you've even considered the boob job, the brow lift, the lipo, the dentistry, the chemical peel or the even more pressing items such as the massages, the eye creams, the face creams, the outfit to wear to the gym. And now we're onto that subject, what about the clothes one must wear day to day?

Sleek doesn't come cheap. Not all Sloanes can afford Sleek. And over the past quarter century as divisions in Sloane-land between the Haves and the Have-Nots have broadened, so the appearance of Sloane has polarized. The Sloane tends to fall into two categories: the glossily perfect or the utterly dishevelled. In the global playing field that London is now, the glossily perfect takes it every time.

WHAT HAPPENED?

It used to be that the smarter and richer you were, the more likely you were to wear your gardening clothes – all day. Lady Dorothy Macmillan, bastion of the Sloane world up until her death in 1966, only ever wore her gardening clothes; one's gardening clothes were a stamp of grandeur.

A lot has happened in the past twenty years – particularly in the last ten – which mean that gardening clothes no longer cut it.

Why? Big Bang saw foreigners start to descend on London. London was suddenly

awash with the fabulously well dressed, the fabulously rich and the well, fabulous really. The arrival of the Euro Sloane brought new standards in clothing and food. For the Euro it's simply anathema to dress down let alone to wear clothes that are ripped, worn or stained – the Euro *never* gardened and wasn't going to be fobbed off with a couple of lukewarm lamb noisettes simply because of its Franglais name.

Then of course there was America. Ever since the late 1990s the Sloane has been returning from New York breathless with tales of dermatologists, eyebrow plucking, waxing and grooming. His unkempt ways got him nowhere in New York.

And finally there was Diana, Princess of Wales. She was the first to go all out for Sleek on such a scale and become a style icon.

Today Sleek is uppermost in Sloane minds and so it's become an infinitely desirable Sloane trait. Where previously one was a secretary, a PA, a PR person or, if brainy, something in publishing, these days a Sloane going places wants a career as a stylist, make-up artist, designer, model or muse. Sleek ensures for Sloane the best of all worlds. It is no longer enough to be merely Sloane.

When French and Saunders got themselves up as a pair of country-loving Sloanes to express the standard stoical Sloane approach to life – 'Bloody hell! Bloody boring. Lost this bloody arm when Bluebell fell on me!' – they were parodying the Sloane of old, tweed to the core. Back then most Sloanes had been bred by resiliant, needs must, war years, stalwart, Queen and Country women. Diana put paid to them.

CAMILLA

Since then even Camilla succumbed to the lure of Sleek despite Diana's role as pioneer. It was always billed as the modelesque princess (representing the modern) versus the frumpy mistress (the old fashioned). Diana glowed like a gym-honed size ten mannequin from every tabloid while the Other Woman smoked, drank and stayed in her jodhpurs all day. Diana's message was clear: I am beautiful. Camilla's message was clearer: I don't give a Sloane how I look as, frankly, there are more important things. Were it not for Diana, Camilla would probably still be in her jodhpurs.

Prince Charles' attitude towards his first wife's interest in clothes was memorable. Looking at the photograph of her at a polo match, lying sprawled on the grass with Harry and wearing a red tee shirt and white jeans, he told her: 'You look like a model.' A put-down with implications like the one he used when she wore a pill-box hat: 'You look like an air hostess.'

Throughout the 1980s and early 1990s, Diana's interest in fashion was alien to the Royal Family, and equally to Tweed Sloane. It was vulgar, American; it was superficial; it was Noove. It was deplorably obsessed about the Wrong Things. Sloane was about backbone, about the person underneath.

A while after Camilla was upgraded from Mistress to Royal Consort some time in 1999, subtle changes were noticed, gathering momentum throughout 2004 and 2005, in the run-up to her wedding: she'd had her teeth fixed; she'd lost weight; her skin was brighter; there were fewer wrinkles around her mouth, eyes and neck. Suddenly the newspapers were taking an interest in Camilla as a style icon – which would have seemed utterly ridiculous during Diana's lifetime.

Interviews began appearing with the 'understated couturiers' Robinson Valentine whom Camilla favoured. These were startling molehills in the croquet lawn of Sloane. Columns were written about the art of ageing gracefully; about the power of understated elegance; about how the mature woman should dress. Much was made of her 'simple, beautifully cut' wedding dress and that show-stopper Philip Treacy hat.

And Camilla's style was coined: 'beautifully cut, understated elegance, topped with a knock-out hat'. Brilliant! And of course the Sloane approved when some weeks later Camilla was spotted again in that wedding dress, this time with the sleeves re-done. Waste not want not is still ingrained in the Sloane: she hadn't lost that good old Sloane thriftiness!

Camilla for Icon! Sloanes wanted to know who did her hair (stylist Hugh Green, whose clients include Joan Collins, and colourist Jo Hansford – the best for blondes!), and were not surprised that her make-up artist was Julia Biddlecombe, someone who can be counted on to know the difference between Hollywood and royalty, being favoured by Lady Helen Taylor, Kate Beckinsale and Jade Jagger. And what about her diet? Camilla saw Dr Mosaraf Ali, an iridologist, who examined the royal eye and prescribed that she cut out wheat and dairy, reduce alcohol, take up yoga and ingest a twice-daily, life-affirming slug of linseed oil.

When it emerged in 2006 that her hairdressing bill was £3000 a month, her husband resolutely stood by her. Within just a few years, Camilla has become a fixture on Best Dressed lists. She's applauded by international style-makers such as Karl Lagerfeld – 'She's the life of the party!' – and Anna Wintour, editor of *American Vogue*, who considers her so glamorous 'it makes your jaw drop!'

In 2006 Camilla did a photo shoot with Mario Testino (whose most famous subject was Diana, Princess of Wales). 'The Duchess of Cornwall is a very good-looking woman,' was his verdict.

The new Sleek Camilla has such cred that in 2005 when she named the Burberry designer Christopher Bailey her favourite, the chav-blighted label perked up.

Unfortunately America, with its absolute standard of scientific beauty hasn't endorsed the Camilla look, variously pronouncing her fat, frumpy, old, and once, memorably, as 'packing the stylistic punch of a dilapidated Yorkshire pudding'.

PLUM SYKES

America is in a different league when it comes to Sleek. And as more Sloanes go to New York and more New Yorkers arrive in London, new standards of Sleek are being set over here. The fact is that to Yanks, even the cleanest Sloane looks dirty.

Brit It-Girl and novelist Plum Sykes came back from New York and, as Prometheus brought fire, she brought news that things were different over there. When she arrived in New York in 1997 she was 'amazed' by how straight everyone's eyebrows were. Her own are now half the width they once were. As are the brows of most of Sloane-land. Her wardrobe underwent a similar honing, from 'London flea market' to cashmere, tailored skirts and polished boots. These days she takes photographs of herself in the fitting room before she'll contemplate buying anything, 'otherwise how will you know how you'll look in party photographs?'

She lives Sleek and she writes about it. Her first novel, *Bergdorf Blondes*, inhabits a New York teeming with PAPs (Park Avenue Princesses), PHs (Prospective Husbands), and 'ana' girls. As the author explained: 'Someone once said to me, "Plum, you're so ana!" I was like, "Anna Wintour?" She said, "No, you're completely anorexic! I worship it!"'

CUT-OUT-AND-KEEP CHECKLIST FOR THE BRITISH SLOANE IN NEW YORK

- ❑ Eyebrow wax every thirteen days
- ❑ Nostril wax every thirteen days
- ❑ Brazilian bikini wax every thirteen days
- ❑ Dermatologist once a week
- ❑ Facial once a week
- ❑ Highlights every thirteen days
- ❑ Manicure and pedicure once a week

PLUM ON GROOMING

- 'In the UK the Queen and your cleaning lady dress the same way.'
- Less is more (hair that is, apart of course from the cascade of silk tresses springing from your head).
- Beauty is not a prerequisite for looking good.
- A hair iron makes a lot of difference: look at Chelsea Clinton.
- Clear skin should not be underestimated: acne is a medical problem.
- In New York, Kate Moss is considered dirty.
- Botox is therapy.

THE SHAPE OF THINGS

The shape of the female Sloane in Britain has changed beyond all recognition since 1982 when her natural state was a size ten to fourteen pear-shape decked in pie-crust frills, corduroy dirndl and flats.

The Sloane has lost a stone and a half, her body is gym honed and her hair is long and messily styled. She skips meals and cares much more about how she'll look in a bikini than sharing a jolly lasagne and lashings of red with friends (of course she still claims 'I eat like a horse!').

THE SLOANE MODEL

Prince Charles might have insulted Diana by telling her, 'You look like a model!', but that was the late 1980s. For a Sloane today, hearing one looks like a model is nothing but good. And modelling is a serious career for any Sloane. Indeed, Capital VIP (see Party Sloane) entices young Sloanes to its parties by advertising the presence of spotters from Models 1.

A couple of rules apply: it's still best for the Sloane to say she got into the industry 'by accident' and it's imperative that she has other strings to her bow. No Naomis or Kates here! To just be a model is not quite the thing.

POSH MODELS OF THE LAST DECADE

SOPHIE DAHL: The granddaughter of author Roald Dahl and the inspiration for the helper in his *The BFG*, Sophie got into modelling 'by accident' and went on to become famous all over the world. She's also published several short stories and a novella, *The Man with the Dancing Eyes*.

JODIE KIDD: The supermodel great-granddaughter of Lord Beaverbrook supplements the adrenalin from modelling (Chloé, Yves St Laurent, Chanel) with polo and then motor racing. These days she's seen more often in a boiler suit than on the runway: 'I don't buy *Vogue*… I buy *Auto Trader*,' says Jodie, who is part of the Maserati team.

IRIS PALMER: The granddaughter of the Duchess of Devonshire and one-time face of Chanel and Lacroix announced in 2004 that she was 'not interested in clothes' and that 'the people are all so boring', and left fashion to pursue various new careers. These included being a painter, a trapeze artist in the circus, and editor-at-large of the now-defunct anti-fashion magazine *Cheap Date*.

HONOR FRASER: The sister of the 16th Lord Lovat, Honor was a reluctant model but was encouraged by her cousin, the late stylist Isabella Blow. Between shoots she worked as a columnist for Scottish mag *Spectrum* and now runs an art gallery, Honor Fraser Inc., in Venice, California.

JASMINE GUINNESS: The great-granddaughter of Diana Mitford and part of the stout-brewing family, Jasmine grew up on a farm wanting to be a writer. Instead she settled for being a supermodel and has since opened a toy shop specializing in nostalgia, Honeyjam, on Portobello Road, where she works between modelling assignments.

STELLA TENNANT: The granddaughter of the Duke and Duchess of Devonshire, Stella is a sculptor who 'got into modelling by accident' and went on to become Karl Lagerfeld's muse and front a Burberry advertising campaign. Now married to a photographer and the mother of four children, she's looking forward to getting back into sculpting.

THE SLOANE FACELIFT

The days when snaggly teeth were a mark of superiority – 'people need to know me, irrespective of my teeth' – are gone. It's a competitive, cruel world out there, and merely being Sloane is no longer sufficient protection. Sloane teeth are straightening and whitening up, especially in London.

The Sloane facelift is a delicate thing. It's not like Joan Rivers', and a good surgeon's number is not a number to be passed around – not even to one's closest girlfriends. It's a private matter between a Sloane and his or her surgeon. When friends say how marvellous one's looking, it's best to leave it at that. The Sloane would still rather people didn't know that one had spent money on one's appearance.

Sloane Procedures

- Post-partum boob job
- Bottom and thigh lipo
- Isolagen regeneration shots
- Teeth whitening
- Brow lift
- Lower face and neck lift (for the jowls)

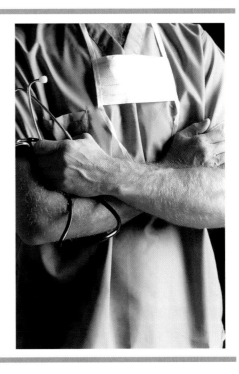

THE SLEEK MALE

The male Sloane took to Sleek somewhat more slowly than his female counterpart. It's really only since the millennium that he's started to open up about his interest in hairdressers, waxing and treatments, massage, moisturisers and botox.

That is not to say that all Sloane men are now Sleek. The ranks are still firmly divided into Thumping Sloanes – who describe themselves as 'astonished that it's possible in this day and age to make a living out of pulling out another person's pubic hair!' (see Thumping Sloane) – and the rather more modern Sloanes who can see on which side their bread is buttered. Modern Sloanes believe that moisturizing one's face is not necessarily bad, common, queer or foreign, particularly in the light of the fact that one may be looking to re-marry later on in life. They can no longer deny the appeal that the coiffed, tweaked, metrosexual Euro Sloane (see Euro Sloane) holds for the sleek, luscious and hotly desirable Party Sloane (see Party Sloane) on the dance floor at Boujis. The fact is that today's sleek Sloanette will desert the unkempt, red faced, pack-minded Thumper in favour of the man with the champagne who clearly looks after his body.

For the Sleek male it's imperative to get massages, have one's back waxed, use a good eye cream, ensure one's eyebrows are attended to, acquire a sun bed, go to the gym and eat healthily.

How things change! Less than a decade ago, the *uber*-Sleek man in London was laughed out of town Now only fools think it's OK to walk out of the shower leaving one's hair au naturel. This is the decade – if you want to get ahead – to take a stand with your appearance. Any Sloane who's going places does. Recently Ben Elliot (see Turbo Sloane) featured in *Vanity Fair*'s regular grooming column, 'My Stuff'. The world wanted to know which face creams and shampoos the Duchess of Cornwall's nephew uses.

TIM JEFFERIES

Tim trail blazed a Sleek path which the male Sloane in London has followed. The Green Shield Stamp heir is on every Best Dressed list going and thanks to his immaculate elegance, his exes include the world's most beautiful women: Claudia Schiffer, Inés Sastre and Kylie Minogue.

Jefferies' tips: He's particular about watches. 'When I meet someone for the first time, I always check out their shoes, their suit and their watch.' He went on to say that he was currently 'awaiting delivery of a platinum IWC regulator, which is an elegant and understated watch for evening wear. But if I'm going to the beach, for example, I would probably wear my Rolex Submariner or a Panerai.' It's all about attention to detail.

THE EURO SLOANE

Euro Sloanes hit London after Big Bang in 1986. They have remained ever since – with their titles, intriguing (or improbable) lineages, estates and castles-on-the-continent – an era in which London overtook New York as the financial capital of the world.

Rich, sophisticated and a formidable party animal, the immaculate Euro Sloane cared about everything from the amount of hair on his chest to the colour of his bedroom walls. Compared with his British counterpart – who drank too much; was frequently boorish, ungallant and consistently red of face; spoke only one language; and was parochial, unsophisticated and more than likely gay (or so it appeared to Euro Sloane who noted, with disgust, Sloane's marathon drinking sessions exclusively in the company of men) – he seemed like a different species.

He *is* a different species. So is the Euro Sloane actually a Sloane? No. Not in the traditional sense. He has no love of farmers, wellington boots or Agas. Nor is he especially keen on London weekends which evaporate in alcohol. He has, however, had a great effect on his British counterpart, with whose life his own is entwined. Not only does he employ the British Sloane but also he has bought up much of stucco-fronted former Sloanedom, thereby putting the squeeze on the Sloane in his habitual stamping grounds.

IN THE BEGINNING

From the beginning British Sloane was aware of Euro Sloane's pitiful limitations: he was a poof (tassels on his shoes), he was ostentatious (spoke four languages, when anyone knew that only English mattered), almost certainly had a bogus title (like 'von' Ribbentrop: 'bloody champagne salesman,' as Sloane's father pointed out), wore jewellery (perhaps inevitable, given that he was obviously a poof), couldn't play cricket and had never rowed or played rugby. Sloane labelled him Eurotrash. The name stuck and is even used today ('Dublin has Euro Cash, London has Eurotrash.')

EUROTRASH

The term Eurotrash was coined by New Yorkers in the early 1980s when titled Europeans hit Manhattan. It is said to have been first used in 1983 by society columnist Taki Theodoracopulos (himself of impeccable Euro credentials, being the son of a Greek shipping magnate, with an infusion of Teutonic blood from his mother's side, and contentedly un-married to Princess Alexandra von Schönberg). Taki explained that he had first heard 'Euro Trash' in 1980, applied to 'very rich Milanese who came here [to New York] and used up everyone's drugs'.

The Euro Sloane is Eurotrash no longer. Alongside his linguistic flair and smorgasbord of titles, the Euro Sloane – schooled in Switzerland, outfitted in Paris and Italy and sometimes even Jermyn Street. Consequently, these days in the City it pays the British Money Sloane to get on with the Euro Sloane. And the Euro Sloane, often against his better instincts, occasionally needs to 'like' the British Sloane.

HOW TO SPOT HIM:

EURO HANDLES

Look for Baron, Count, Prince, Princess, Graf, Grafin, Archduke, Infanta. Anything with a 'von' prefix. Anything starting King or Queen, invariably referring to an obsolescent dynasty in a country/ principality/state which no longer exists (assuming that it ever did). Keep eyes peeled – on the next rung down – for the names of once-great leaders of state, shipping tycoons, nation-makers. Be prepared to embrace names such as Bourbon, Hanover, Habsburg, Bismarck, Niarchos.

OTHER EURO GIVEAWAYS

- Loafers without socks
- Keeps sunglasses on during lunch and at weddings (and certain funerals)
- Hermes and Gucci
- Has done the Cresta Run
- Displays impressive lack of knowledge of anything to do with popular culture: *Big Brother*; TV of any sort; Britney Spears
- Impeccable English spoken with a 'multilingual' accent

- Wears a signet ring – possibly two – and/or wedding ring (applies to both male and female Euro Sloanes)
- Male stands when a woman enters the room
- Female Euro Sloane hands empty glass to any passing man, confident that it will be refilled; allows someone else to pay for dinner without offering to 'go Dutch'
- Spends weekends on planes, flying to weddings
- Mother. Untitled at birth, daughter of soap manufacturer or, equally likely, owner of chain of Iberian abattoirs. Is horrified by the ranks of marauding British Sloanes around Bibi, her daughter who lives in a flat off the King's Road
- He is called Tassilo, Ludo, Stefan, Riccardo, Christian; she is called Bibi, Anna, Maria, Anna-Maria or something weirdly Scandinavian

WHAT IS HE DOING
IN LONDON?

The Male Euro Sloane is in London for one reason: money (possibly the preservation of – thanks to the 'resident, non-dom' rule, he pays no tax on any investment income he brings into the UK; more likely the accumulation of – via the City, a term which no longer signifies geographical location, only rapacious intent; but, most probably, for both.)

Although unlikely to have been at school here – there are exceptions, of course, quite often at Ampleforth and various other Benedictine institutions – he might have arrived for university to study economics, PPE, law or business at Oxford or Cambridge or, more probably, at the LSE, UCL or King's (the Euro Sloane likes to be in London).

He will demonstrate a natural hunger for business from a young age. This, plus his mastery of more than GCSE French, will assure him a head start over British Sloanes. Euro Sloane tends to skip the tedium of conventional career advancement, progressing quickly to a hedge fund or venture capital firm in St James's, though some suffer the large investment banks in return for immense rewards.

In this world of turbo financing, everyone wants the Euro Sloane. Being cosmopolitan by instinct and upbringing – *pace* the defiant insularity of the British Sloane – the Euro Sloane is more willing to attempt negotiations with money-makers of whom the Brit is more wary (the Iranians, the Russians, the Sheikhs). The Brit Sloane is aware of this. He is prepared to make tactical concessions to his rival, possibly inviting him shooting or – better – to a cricketing weekend, during which the Euro Sloane can be patronized for his brave but hopeless performance, with the bonus that he may suffer humiliating injury.

The female Euro Sloane in London is waiting for male Euro Sloane to accumulate 'enough' money. There remains the danger that this will never happen, but the interim years, or decades, offer consolations, notably the chance to have cosmetic and reconstructive work done on the Euro house (perhaps in The Vale (Chelsea), or Tregunter Road, or The Boltons), as well, of course, as on herself. Female Euro Sloane will never be neglected at a polo match.

THE BRITISH SLOANE ON THE EURO SLOANE AND THE EFFECTS OF THE EURO SLOANE ON THE BRITISH SLOANE AND PARTICULARLY HER MOTHER

Not only is the Euro Sloane bloody good at business, but he's also more than bloody likely to have a bloody big estate somewhere in Austria or Greece or Bavaria.

On top of that it's more than likely that he'll be the richest person partying at Boujis, Volstead, Cuckoo, Chinawhite – though not necessarily at Annabel's – being blessed with family money and/or a very well-paid job; he will undoubtedly be the most charming person there, as well as the one appearing to have the best time. He and female Euro Sloane will be beautifully dressed; they will move beautifully across the dance floor; they may also be the most beautiful people present. Whether he is or not depends entirely on whether his father opted for the soap manufacturer/abattoir owner's daughter or stuck rigidly to the in-breeding policy of the past seven centuries. If the latter, the male Euro Sloane will display a disturbingly prominent Adam's apple, a perilously narrow forehead and exopthalmic eyes, and will clutch a bottle of champagne throughout the evening. Female Euro Sloane – if similarly so constructed – will never be seen in London, spending her entire adult life in missionary work in Africa or South America.

EFFECT ON FEMALE SLOANE

The British Sloane who has decided that she'd like to marry outside the box and unite with Euro is not alone. There's just something about him… He's so utterly charming. He always calls when he says he will and is always on time. Plus there's the style with which he takes her out: he always gets a table, and always makes sure she's got a drink.

His manners are impeccable. He lights her cigarettes, opens doors, offers seats. And obviously, her parents – her mother, anyway – absolutely adore him. The Sloane's Mother reflects that not only is he a prince, but he's a prince who kisses her hand every time they meet. The Sloane's Father points out that there's no primogeniture on the continent, where titles are handed out with the Alpen, and, had the Sloane family been established on the other side of the Channel, it would by now be loaded with at least a brace of titles, and quite possibly a significant claim to a throne, rather than making do with the double-barrel it acquired in 1890.

THE EURO SLOANE ON THE BRITISH SLOANE

Unfortunately, the Euro Sloane holds rather a dim view of his British counterpart. To the Euro, the British Sloane seems badly dressed, is descended as often as not from some brewing or sausage-making family – on his father's side – and tends not to know when he's had enough to drink. His manners are erratic: should he be at the bar in Boujis, he's probably buying himself a drink while the woman he's with is left to fend for herself.

There's no getting around it: the Brit is unsophisticated, monolingual and primitive, especially in his prurient and disapproving interest in the love affairs of others. *Mon dieu!* Anyone would think you were meant to stick to one woman for the rest of your life!

So, when in London, like tends to stick with like and the Euro Sloane prefers the company of other Euro Sloanes.

PARTY REPUTATION

The Euro Sloane has a well-deserved reputation for knowing how to party, especially in the Schloss belt of Mittel Europe. An eighteenth, a twenty-first, a wedding: each triggers, three-day, fully monogrammed extravaganzas (with initials on everything from the towels to the table linen to the cars sent to collect guests from the airport). Brunch the following day is an intrinsic part of the Euro party, as is the promiscuous use of firearms – much to Brit Sloane's delight – either boar ('free range pig,' says the Brit Sloane) or an extended blast at the clays (clay pigeons).

Euro parties range from the rustic to the unimaginably glamorous, though most combine elements of both. The hosts do not lightly spurn the chance to clamber into Lederhosen and share a hog roast at trestle tables, with musical accompaniment being provided by the local oompah town band (many of whose members work on the Euro Host's estate, as their forebears have done for innumerable generations). One Euro Sloane recalls a party she attended whose theme was Atlantis – the Euro Sloane, in common with all Sloanes, LOVES a theme. Guests moved from one area to another through 'a wall of water' without ever getting wet. Magical.

At a recent eighteenth birthday party held in Germany, guests stayed for three days, two to a room (this, pitiful little Schloss had only thirty-five bedrooms). Entertainments included croquet, tennis and ping-pong tournaments (the Euro loves a competition!); but the undoubted highlight was the sumo wrestling contest staged on monogrammed mats. The theme this time was the *Flintstones*, and guests were supplied with fur, clubs and bones and given an afternoon to construct a costume. Arguably, though, Euro weddings most excite the British Sloane, if only because he – and she – can (legitimately) carry off a trophy from the weekend, invariably a ceramic ashtray, made in Euro Sloane's family factory, on which the bride and groom's names or initials are entwined in a copybook glaze.

The Euro party scene in London is not
dissimilar, though it has to be slightly
scaled down in a nod to metropolitan
constrictions. Take the fortieth
birthday party held for Crown
Prince Pavlos of Greece at his
Chelsea town house in the
summer of 2007. (Greece
abolished its monarchy in 1974;
an irksome but ultimately
inconsequential detail to Prince
Pavlos and his father King
Constantine.) The theme of the
party was Heaven and Hell
and, in typical Euro Sloane
style, there was no stinting on
decorations. Ice sculptures of
angels filled the marquee in the
garden (Heaven), while the
swimming pool in the basement
was surrounded by stilt-walkers
and erotic dancers (Hell).

Festivities raged all night and
recognizable faces emerged at all
hours in varying degrees of
intoxication: some ruddy with
bonhomie, others shouting and
fighting. Lord Frederick Windsor
emerged with a gash to his nose
while Prince Andrew left in
high spirits as the sun came up.

EURO LIVES

The Euro Sloane divides his time between St Tropez, St Moritz, Gstaad (he never skis in Val d'Isère – too many uncouth Brits; or America – too many uncouth Yanks), Mustique, New York, Sardinia, Monaco, Ibiza, Marbella and London, where he usually is in June. Unless of course he works in London and then he's there for somewhat more than just June.

Largely he lives in Chelsea, Mayfair, South Kensington, Notting Hill, Prince of Wales Drive, Belgravia. He loves Belgravia for its quietness and the elegance of all 200 acres of its cream stucco-fronted streets. And he loves Sloane Square and Knightsbridge – little enclaves that buzz with his favourite restaurants, San Lorenzo and Aubaine for extended Sunday brunches (and to see who is shopping at Chanel).

But the truth is the Euro Sloane loves more than anywhere Belgravia's Elizabeth Street: Baker and Spice for coffee and croissants; Jeroboams for wine and cheese; and the delectable Poilâne for traditional French bread.

TURBO
SLOANE

Meet
George

George, thirty-four, spends half his time in New York half his time in London and half his time in Dubai. But three halves don't make a whole! Actually they can when it comes to George – he crosses the International Date Line so frequently that as far as he's concerned there are nine days to the average week.

He set up Jet Set, Go three years ago. And now, with his partner James, he runs a fleet of fourteen private jets. And helicopters, too. The move into choppers was a good one and it's now a core part of the business: Jet Set, for example, flew all the major stars in for all the UK festivals last year. Agents and managers like the company; it's geared up to handle the most sensitive client requirements and that's why Jet Set is on speed-dial for a surprisingly broad sector of the population: rock stars, footballers, department store owners, oligarchs and plutocrats. The one thing uniting this tribe is money and because of the quantities involved, most of George's clients are household names.

Perhaps it's not surprising that Sloanes rarely use Jet Set, not even the few who could afford it. It's just not really Sloane. George views this attitude as similar to that of the average black cab driver: take a cab himself? Never! Ridiculous waste of money.

So what gave George the idea for Jet Set? First and foremost – and in fact, second and third – the urge to make money. He decided long ago that he was not going to fade away like his father had – or worse still, become notorious the way co-founder James' father had. The poor guy, a former officer, was caught embezzling money and, because he was Lord Justice of the County and a decorated soldier, he had made the front page of several newspapers. And all because he was having trouble – after the Lloyds' debacle – putting four children through school.

Plus, George found it upsetting that so much serious cash had descended – Russian, Euro, Yank, Middle Eastern – on Sloane London. Who were these people who were buying up the stucco squares of Chelsea? Buying up the football clubs? Creating this new London awash with Cristal, fabulous restaurants and helipads? And why wasn't George getting a slice?

So, six years ago, with James (his father may have been disgraced but he still had useful contacts at various airstrips around the country) and with money from James' godfather, and cash from two school friends (trust funds requiring separate bank vaults) they leased four nine-seater Falcon jets. George was working in the music industry at the time and knew (oh, how he knew!) the trouble musicians were having finding the right company to ferry them around. A company which understood the artistic temperament as well as the level of service demanded by the very rich was desperately needed and thus Jet Set, Go was born.

Jet Set is on speed-dial for a surprisingly broad sector of the population: rock stars, footballers, department store owners, oligarchs and plutocrats.

George eats, thinks and drinks Jet Set. He has done since its inception. When he first started out, he used to entertain friends with stories of his clients: the Russian oligarch – yes, him! – who booked a jet from Tokyo to London. For the flight he requested an exercise bike of the type used for spinning. With that he booked a trained instructor who could take him through a fifty-minute work out. He also requested two female masseuses plus, of course, the usual Dom Perignon and a selection of sashimi from Nobu, London. Hello? You're in Tokyo! No, he wouldn't be moved: the sashimi must be from Nobu, London. And so, a couple of hours into the flight, he'd had the sashimi, he'd done his spinning and was now drinking Dom Perignon whilst being massaged somewhere over Iran. And then the whole thing fell apart when he made some excessive demands of the masseuses. It was known as wanting a 'happy ending', George learned later when he talked to a friend at Quintessentially. 'All the good hotels have panic buttons in their spa massage rooms,' Tom had said. But George hadn't known that then. The girls spent the remainder of the journey locked in the cockpit with the pilot while the Russian passed out on the massage table. Unfortunately, George was unaware that the new girlfriend of one of his friends worked for a UK tabloid; that weekend the story surfaced in three Sunday papers.

If he's so brilliant at servicing clients enroute, why not take a slice of the pie at the other end too?

Discretion is everything now and George won't even tell his mother who uses Jet Set. The leak didn't seem to have bothered the Russian though, who sent flowers to the girls, flowers to the pilot and continues to use Jet Set to this day.

George's latest venture is hotels. If he's so brilliant at servicing clients enroute, why not take a slice of the pie at the other end too? Jet Set is a brand associated all over the world with the top end in fully serviced, low-key luxury. And so, capitalizing on that, their first boutique hotel and spa opened in the Meatpacking District of Manhattan last month. It's cool, it's urban, it's taupe and the Jet Set helipad on top of the building already guarantees a plutocratic clientele.

The main reason that Jet Set is performing so brilliantly is that George modelled it on an American company where service and customer care is everything. Half of his staff work in customer relations. Their skills? Smoothing ruffled feathers and last minute fixes.

Thanks to Jet Set, George is one of the best-connected men in London, and the simple truth is that a lot of people want to keep him onside. It's been a long time since he had trouble getting a table anywhere. He's a fixture on all Lists on both sides of the Atlantic: Most Eligible, Most Successful, Most Entrepreneurial, Oh and Best Dressed which really makes his mother laugh: for about four years in his teens he refused to wear anything except a pair of orange corduroy dungarees.

George is currently single. It's not that he doesn't have girlfriends, just that his life doesn't really allow for having a wife and family. That's not to say there's any shortage of contenders willing to step up to the breach and share the house in Notting Hill and the apartment in New York's West Village. The truth is that a woman – now, anyway – would have to play second fiddle to Jet Set, and, as George has

He's the first member of his family to have made a real mark since the Boer War when his great-grandfather derailed a train.

already discovered, it's hard to find a modern woman who will put up with that. His last relationship ended when his girlfriend of only four months ripped his Blackberry out of his hands and threw it into the Serpentine. He could have killed her. It must have cost Jet Set several hundred thousand pounds worth of business. Ever since then George has ensured that all his emails and contacts are automatically backed up.

His parents are slightly bemused by him but they're proud of him too, on some level: after all he's the first member of his family to have made a real mark since the Boer War when his great-grandfather derailed a train. They knew he was unusual when, at the age of fourteen, he dropped his given name of Sebastian in favour of George in homage to his great-grandfather.

His mother says, 'George might be OE but he makes his living as a chauffeur!'

George just laughs, 'I might be a chauffeur Ma, but I'm a damn well-paid one.'

TURBO SLOANE

The Turbo Sloane is the Sloane in Vertical Take-Off. No longer apologetic. No longer iffy about money, this Sloane is not only up to competing in a meritocracy but is the one who's found a turbo-fuelled way of bypassing the whole shebang. Why just compete when you could go stratospheric?

London is the centre of the world and the Turbo Sloane is damned if he's going to allow that to pass him by. Turbo wants the world and he's going to start by reclaiming the City, reclaiming London and then the planet.

This Sloane thinks and acts globally: his plans are not confined to the shores of this Once Great Nation. He might not have a big trust fund (on the other hand he might), but chances are he'll have access to cash and contacts, often in the form of well-placed godparents; trust-funded Old School chums or a by-marriage connection. Unassailed by doubt and with his unstoppable sense of entitlement, he's out to rule the world. Unfazed by Euro, Yank, even Russian billions, Turbo will do whatever it takes – ruthless capitalization on contacts, heroic lies, a dependence on artificial stimulants – in order to get here.

TURBO JETS

NetJets

'Every flight is non-stop. Everyone is polite. You go straight from your house or office to the plane. The cabin is all yours. Take a deep breath – you are, once again, in control of your life.' Offers 'fractional ownership' or a 'Jet Card' which provides 25 hours' flying time. (£50,000 – £150,000 depending on type of aircraft chosen.)

Silverjet

'Business-class carrier': 40 flat beds per plane, every flight is carbon neutral. Transfers: helicopter, chauffeur pick-up or valet parking. New York to London, £1,000 return.

MAXjet

Luxury only cross-Atlantic jet carrier from Stanstead. 100 seats on Boeing 767.

Eos

Luxury only cross-Atlantic jet carrier from Stansted. 40 seats on a Boeing 757. 'We have 21 square feet per seat; BA has just 15 on Club World.'

Welcome to the world of the Turbo Sloane: born out of pressure on family money, forged in the City and through the dotcom boom, he rubs shoulders with bright young sparks and emerges on the other side with 'the idea'. It's about contacts; it's about New York; it's about money and it's about the Turbo doing it for himself.

And more often than not it's about *servicing the Very Rich*: the Turbo is the Sloane turned global butler and is making a fortune out of it. In this world contacts are everything; the Turbo might not have the billions (yet) but the billionaire doesn't have the contacts or the confidence.

FROM THE ASHES RISES THE TURBO

THE BIG BANG

In 1986 the City was deregulated. It went from Empire rockpool to international shark-infested waters almost over night. American banks descended and the City became the centre of the world. Non-doms, foreign money, billionaires: London was known as 'Switzerland on Thames'. It's home to the richest people in the world. It's the hedge fund centre of the world (more cash is managed out of two square miles of Mayfair than in the whole of Germany).

And the shock for the Sloane has been coming to terms with the realization that he – or she – is no longer automatically at the top of the pile. Or indeed anywhere near it. When Lloyds happened, lots of Sloanes fell off the cliff face.

LLOYDS

The Lloyds 'debacle' ruined tens of thousands of Sloanes. Run as a private club with friends of friends signing up – just the kind of thing a Sloane loves – the early days were halcyon and the cheques kept on flying in. Being a Lloyds 'name' in the good years underwrote the children's education and lent a kind of economic royalty. It was for the grand, the rich, the British elite; the Sloane (Camilla Parker Bowles was a name). And then came the late 1980s and asbestos. By the early 1990s many (thanks to unlimited liability) had only the cords they stood up in. Vast tracts of Sloane wealth – mostly belonging to George's father's generation – were wiped out. There are estimated to have been between twenty and thirty Lloyds' related suicides. It is still referred to with downcast eyes and bitterness. 'It was terrible.'

GRANNY

Sloanes have spent the past twenty-five years watching helplessly from Gloucestershire as Granny relinquished her flat in Cadogan Square to a French banker who already owned the flats on either side. He needed Granny's for a bedroom in his lateral conversion. The family's last foothold in Chelsea was eventually sold in 1994 for £350,000. Granny was terribly pleased. She and Peter had bought it as a pied-à-terre – in 1962 for absolutely nothing. Her grandchildren, briefly impressed by granny's small fortune, became obsessed by the bigger one that they might have inherited, had she had the decency to die there. 'It would be worth £1.5 million now, minimum,' George moans. Granny heads happily down to the annex in Glos., after becoming a member of the Sloane Club, which she visits once a month, returning to the country with reports of what a nice lunch she has had. Her grandchildren choke.

THE CALL TO ACTION

The Turbo Sloane is hungry to take back his place on top of the pile. However it's not just London that the Turbo wants to conquer; it's the world.

The Turbo is all about accumulation, not selling to survive, so it's this Sloane who is most critical of his parents' generation and of the Old Sloane who used to baulk at 'money talk'. In fact the very last thing the Turbo would like to be described as – despite his impeccable credentials – is a Sloane. The Turbo is sleeker, cooler, faster and much more expensive. And infinitely better groomed and better dressed. However just because the Turbo has eschewed braces, cords and the Admiral Codrington for New York, gadgets and private jets, does *not* mean he is not a Sloane Ranger. For christ's sake, he's OE in a Savile Row suit with a vintage Rolex, brothers in the Guards, sisters in PR, parents in Gloucestershire and a vocabulary that would never, but never, extend to the word 'toilet'. (In America they think he's Hugh Grant.)

THE SLOANE AND THE DOTCOM

In the late 1990s came the 'dotcom boom'. It looked as though there were millions to be made for not much work, and the young Turbo got a glimpse of what it might be like to have a limitless supply of cash.

It looked like a massive confidence trick: any company with a link to the internet seemed to find itself in the FTSE 100 within weeks. And so the Sloane got involved – wine sites, sports sites, shopping sites, gossip sites, auction sites, betting sites, travel sites. Usually it was someone else's money that got burned, often from US 'incubators' over here looking for a slice of the action in the UK.

Three years later it was all over: billions burned. Most of these businesses hadn't built brands or markets. What had been ecstatically known as B2C ('Business to Consumer') and B2B ('Business to Business') quickly came to mean 'Back to Consulting' and 'Back to Banking' or even 'Back to Bed' as the newly redundant Sloanes returned to their previous lives. The handful of Sloanes that made it were just that, a handful: QXL founder Tim George (City of London, Oxford); Lastminute pair Brent Hoberman (Eton and Oxford) and Martha Lane Fox (Westminster, Oxford and the great niece of the 6th Marquess of Anglesey). Out of the ashes of the dotcom boom however came the Turbo Sloane; beefed up on confidence tricks and hungry for lovely new cash on both sides of the Atlantic. He *knew* it was there.

CONTACTS

It is all about contacts and the Turbo Sloane will nurture and cement any contact to help and promote the business; a relationship with other Turbos on the up will become reassuringly symbiotic.

Take for example the élite concierge club Quintessentially run by the Duchess of Cornwall's nephew Ben Elliot (*uber* Turbo). The company services the incredibly rich and is famous for flying Madonna's favourite tea bags (slippery elm) halfway round the world for her; for getting twenty front row tickets for a Mick Jagger concert on the night of the show; for delivering twelve albino peacocks to Jennifer Lopez; for getting any member into the hottest new restaurant in London, New York, Hong

Kong (twenty-eight countries and counting); and for flying out a set of false eyelashes to a party hostess in St Tropez together with a plastic surgeon, after she had damaged her eyelids ripping out the last pair.

That's all fair enough, but the next question is: would the super-rich celebrity be so keen to sign up to a concierge company founded and run by any old bod? Perhaps. But it didn't harm Ben Elliot, founder of Quintessentially, when he became the Prince of Wales' nephew (Camilla and Elliot's mother, Annabel, are sisters), and

consequently he is now a step-cousin of William and Harry. Ben Goldsmith, who is married to Kate Rothschild and is Zac Goldsmith's brother, was involved at the inception of Quintessentially. Elliot shares an office in New York with Nick Jones in his New York SoHo House in the Meatpacking District. As far as Nick Jones's connections go… there are few in media-land who would not be delighted to take his call. And so here we have connections to the very highest echelons in the parallel worlds of royalty, plutocracy and showbiz. This would explain why Quintessentially is doing spectacularly well as 'the UK's greatest export'.

Another interesting web of Turbo connections spins around the film *Four Weddings and a Funeral.*

THE SLOANE LOOP

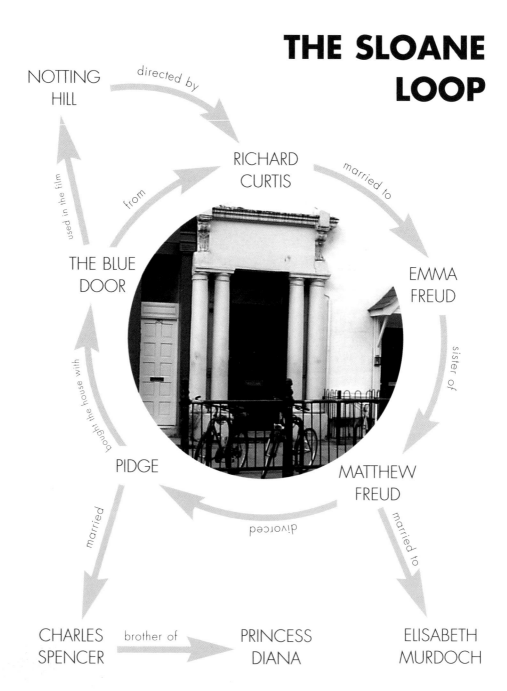

NOTTING HILL

directed by

RICHARD CURTIS

married to

EMMA FREUD

used in the film

from

THE BLUE DOOR

sister of

bought the house with

PIDGE

divorced

MATTHEW FREUD

married

married to

CHARLES SPENCER

brother of

PRINCESS DIANA

ELISABETH MURDOCH

This was the first convincingly Sloane film, about Sloanes and by Sloanes. It managed to celebrate Sloanes, not just to themselves but to the world. And for the first time for decades the Sloane became a national treasure, especially Hugh Grant . Its sister film – or sequel – *Notting Hill*, demonstrates the Sloane contact book at work: Harrovian Richard Curtis wrote the script which was then edited by his wife, Emma Freud. Meanwhile Emma Freud's brother Matthew Freud divorced his wife 'Pidge'. Freud then married Elisabeth Murdoch, while a newly divorced Charles Spencer – Princess Diana's brother and the Queen's godson – married Pidge. When Charles and Pidge came out as a couple at the premiere of *Notting Hill*, it transpired that Pidge owned the house with the blue door which belonged to Hugh Grant in the film. She had bought it from Richard Curtis who is married to Emma Freud, the sister of Matthew Freud. Confusing, yes, but the simple message is that there's no harm in knowing a lot of very useful people.

As with Quintessentially, here we have royalty (well nearly anyway: Charles Spencer), the Freuds and the daughter of the UK's most powerful media baron. We also have of course, Matthew Freud, who can't really be classed merely as a 'Freud' as he is by far and away this nation's best-connected man; he has links with Mandelson, Cameron, Campbell and everyone who's anyone in media and showbiz.

TURBO JOBS

Introductions networking or 'supper club' introductions

Chauffeurs private jet, helicopter

Concierge services (including gaining access to clubs, bars and restaurants for clients or merely showing Hollywood actresses a good time in London)

Fast Food posh take-away

Catalogue shopping What? Yes, catalogue shopping

NOBS DO YOBS' JOBS

The Turbo Sloane is tapping into the service industry and is setting up companies to service the *uber* Rich. These nobs are doing yobs' jobs and getting paid a fortune for it. Forget the antiquarian booksellers and the wine merchants. Instead the Turbo Sloane is master-turned-servant.

The Servant (1963) stars James Fox (Tony, the master of the house and something of a playboy) and Dirk Bogarde (Barrett, the servant). The film opens with Tony, the ultimate master, treating Barrett as a virtual slave. Slowly but surely Barrett takes control, using Tony's sister (Sarah Miles) as bait. Eventually Tony loses his supremacy in the household, the roles are subverted and Tony and Barrett find themselves head-to-head in a dubious homoerotic battle which, it seems, will go the servant's way.

Turbo doesn't see himself as part of the servant class. Obviously he is not as rich as his client, yet, but thanks to his no-nonsense, Sloane upbringing, he secretly thinks his clients requests are insecure and absurd. But it's also thanks to his upbringing that he's so fantastically polite and diplomatic towards them.

CATALOGUE SHOPPING

Today's catalogue shopper is as likely to be a Cash Rich Time Poor Sloane as a Littlewoods devotee whiling away a dreary afternoon choosing bedsocks with elephant motifs (see Chav Sloane for a discussion of Trinny and Susannah). Equally, the catalogue retailer is most likely to be an enterprising Turbo Sloane who is capitalizing on her address book and contacts, first to understand exactly what these CRTP Sloanes want and second, to assemble the correct and invaluable core mailing list. As the Catalogue Turbo knows, the address book is all important.

BODEN

Old Etonian Johnnie Boden left Oxford (Oriel), went into the City, left after five years and started the Boden catalogue. In 1991 it featured just eight items perfect for the budget conscious Sloane (as he was then): boxer shorts, cords and a selection of shirts. The first collection sold spectacularly well: £600,000. And it has continued to sell: in 2006 sales came in at £125 million, up £23 million from 2005, with thirty per cent of turnover coming from America (Boden launched over there in 2002). Each catalogue is a virtual Sloane Ranger handbook: the clothes are good, solid, all-rounders – bright, easy to wear, well-cut, hard-wearing and inspired by the American

preppy market. As Johnnie Boden didn't have enough money to hire models for the first few years, his friends stood in for him: Old Etonians, architects and PRs enjoying a ruddy outdoor life, with captions like:'Henry is an architect who loves his Labrador, Jasper.' Cosy, familiar, healthy.

The website is equally chummy. It lists a few of Johnnie's favourite things: 'No agenda here, just some things that I really, really like: books – *Anna Karenina*, *Pride and Prejudice*, *Decline and Fall*; dogs – Jack Russell, Norfolk terrier, lurcher; music – Morcheeba, Keane, Radiohead.'

Always interested in clothes, his first foray into fashion came when as a young man he wrote a style piece for *Harpers & Queen*. It was a source of some embarrassment to his parents Lt Col. and Mrs Boden, as Johnnie explained in an interview: 'My father was very cross about it, actually. Just didn't understand it. He thought fashion was ghastly, unmanly, not a proper job. What was wrong with a nice blue blazer?'

THE WHITE COMPANY

Christian Rucker was a beauty editor at *Harpers & Queen*. Trying to kit out a house she realized she couldn't find anyone offering plain white linen, white towels and, well, white furnishings. So she founded the White Company in 1994 in her boyfriend's – Nick Wheeler, the founder of Tyrwhitt Shirts – attic. This was an inspired move as the Sloane hates naff coloured towels and there was a marked shortage of anything white for sale.

The Problem with Laura Ashley

Ever since Laura Ashley was taken over by Malaysians ('they haven't a clue!'), the Sloane has been left in limbo as far as decorating needs go; after all this was the most reliable shop for cheap, class-correct fabrics and clothes for Sloanes. The canny Turbo however spotted this need and stepped up to mobilize her address book. Decorating and furnishing catalogues are now big business for Turbo Sloanes.

In 1994 Rucker produced and shot the first catalogue: 'I wasn't fazed since I had plenty of experience of organizing photo shoots on magazines. The only problem was: who could I send them to? Obviously friends of friends and all my mother's friends… but that was about it!' It proved enough however and Rucker is now worth an estimated £40 million, with over 625,000 customers; the White Company produces ten brochures a year, operates a highly successful website and has seventeen shops.

In other words, it helps if friends of friends and friends of mother's are well placed to shop.

OKA

Annabel Astor, David Cameron's mother-in-law 'has a talent for designing a room that works and looks good. She builds a room up layer by layer, so that antiques sit happily alongside new accessories. In 1999 she established OKA, an interiors mail order catalogue selling rattan furniture. Shoppers can choose between ottomans and *chaises longues* in shades of serenity, or silk taffeta curtains in duck-egg blue stripes. It was an instant hit. Demand has been extensive and OKA currently has nine shops (Notting Hill, Edinburgh, Wiltshire – all hotbeds of Sloane living) as well as the catalogue and internet. As a serious Turbo, Lady Astor is not shy about her relationship with her enterprising son-in-law, the leader of the Conservative party.

MAIL-ORDER SPECS

Anyone can have a brilliant idea but it's the cash that counts. Prince William's good friend Jamie Murray Wells who runs his mail order glasses business from a disused stable in his parents' Gloucestershire farmyard was a millionaire by the age of twenty-one. As he explained: 'The first round of funding came from friends and family.'

FAST FOOD

Patrick Reeves and Rohan Blacker set up Deliverance in 1997 after identifying a gap in the takeaway market; what was needed was good quality, fresh food that could be delivered anywhere in London within forty minutes. From sushi to Salade Niçoise. Soon those working late in the City and exhausted Sloanes across the capital developed a taste for it.

THE FIRST ROUND OF FUNDING CAME FROM FRIENDS AND FAMILY.

THE IMPORTANCE OF FRIENDS WITH MONEY TO INVEST

It's helpful if the Turbo knows people with money to spare and who want to invest. One such serial investor is Ben Goldsmith. He's said to have around £300 million and, along with his brother Zac, is a very good man for the Turbo to know. Investments to date include Mark Von Westonholtz's All Star Lanes Bowling; Ben Elliot's Quintessentially; James Reatchlous' Luxury Publishing Ltd; as well as other interests of friends and family including various bars and members' clubs around London. And of course no Goldsmith portfolio would be complete without an ecological project or two: Ben Goldsmith's range from a luxury eco resort in Romania to Belu, a bottled water with a zero carbon footprint.

THE IMPORTANCE OF MARKETING

The Turbo Sloane knows the importance of marketing. Besides having a brimming address book, the Turbo will have no compunction about marketing his or her connections with anyone important including the dead, royalty, children and the plutocracy through whatever means are at his disposal. The Turbo Sloane doesn't have the old inhibitions about being pushy and indiscreet (apart from when it comes to his client list, of course). After all, life is short and he can't afford that old false modesty.

They will also spend a fortune on web designs and websites as well as on web names. Pat Reeves and Rohan Blacker, Turbo Sloanes who went on to found sofa.com, spent a chunk of their start-up budget on the web name because no matter how fabulous your product and no matter how cheap, the Turbo knows that a hot internet brand is the way to give a business lift-off.

NYLON

The successful Turbo lives a New York/London existence. He's a boy racer and if the business hasn't expanded to the States yet, he's certainly looking into it. The Turbo will spend his time hanging out in SoHo House and at the Mercer with the other Turbos in the enclave of New York they're turning into Little Britain. Then he may have breakfast at Pastis; brunch at the Spotted Pig; lunch at Macelleria (steak); afternoon tea at the Chocolate Bar and then back to SoHo House to reunite with the other Turbos and on to Bungalow 8.

PRIVATE JETS

The Turbo Sloane loves private jets, especially if he isn't paying (he usually isn't). He's constantly weighing up various schemes: is it better to buy flying hours or do a timeshare with friends? Going skiing of course the only option is to charter a jet for oneself and eleven friends – after all, divided between twelve

there's nothing in it! And what feels better than the cool softness of proper calf leather beneath the buttock? The Turbo loves anything leaving from Stansted, Luton, Farnborough, Northholt or Biggin Hill.

CLUB-BABLE TURBO

The Turbo is very Club orientated. Not only setting up exclusive clubs but also being members of each other's clubs. No Turbo worth his salt, however, would actually pay to join a club. *Au contraire*, true Turbos are begged by other Turbos to join: a Turbo's life revolves around being welcomed into places about which others can only dream.

WHO IS HARRY BECHER?

Harry Becher's job is to make the lives of celebrities 'as easy as possible'. He works 'with' Quintessentially and indeed set up its LA office. However, he is single-handedly and officially London's top Fixer. If Scarlett Johansson is photographed leaving Boujis or if Mischa Barton is seen leaving Nobu on the arm of a protective blond man – suit, shirt, signet ring and glistening white trainers, (I'm no wage monkey!) who is holding back the paps – it's likely to be Harry Becher. 'I love people and I love partying. I know every doorman on every door in every club in London.' And what is it that makes a good Fixer? 'It's about knowing your customer – you put the New York businessman in Claridges, the LA film director in the Sanderson.' And what does London's top Fixer do to relax? 'I do have time out sometimes in Hampshire, but I check my messages every two hours.'

Turbo Club Membership

Clubs a Turbo should be a member of, or at least, 'work closely with':

Quintessentially
Boujis (the private members lounge)
Soho House (plus Soho House, New York)
The Electric
NetJets
Annabel's

WHO IS SERENA COOK?

The Harry Becher of Ibiza. She met Jade Jagger through an ex-boyfriend, and Jade was desperate for a cook. 'I had just closed Deli Organic with my friend Sheherazade Goldsmith [wife of Zac Goldsmith],' recalls Serena, 'and I thought, "Why not?" Two days later, I was buying up all the fresh fish in Ibiza's markets for a dinner party for eighteen of Jade's friends – I was terrified.'

That was a few years ago and Serena has now moved to Ibiza and can get anything for a client on 'the white island': the best table at Sa Capella, at Pacha or a boat to Formentera as well as offering advice as to where an individual should be seen, when, with whom and on which beach. 'Fixing in Ibiza has to be the easiest thing in the world – it's hot, hedonistic and beautiful. People are here to have fun. I often find myself driving across the island, repeating, "I love my life, I love my life!" Who wouldn't?'

THE ART DEALER

Just because you are phenomenally rich, does not mean that you are automatically blessed with taste: this is another opening for the Turbo Sloane.

Old Etonian Jay Jopling son of Michael, former Tory Cabinet Minister, (who remarked of Michael Heseltine: 'The trouble with Michael is that he had to buy all his furniture'), works tirelessly to redress the cash balance between the New Rich and the Turbo Sloane through his White Cube galleries. David Beckham for example is a client (Posh got a Damien Hirst 'Butterflies' for her fourth wedding anniversary). Elton John is also a client along with many other 'self-made' souls. Jopling is selling taste at an impressive premium, as guaranteed by himself, by Eton, by the establishment, by the Brit Art community and by White Cube.

And how better to emphasize the combination of taste and background than by opening the doors to your family's twelfth-century Gloucestershire castle – once a favourite house of Henry VIII – to host an art fair? Mollie Dent-Brocklehurst, director of the Gagosian Gallery, London (sister outfit of New York's most cutting-edge dealership) did just this in 2005 and it was so successful that the Sudely Castle Art Fair is now a crucial annual event.

WHERE TURBO LIVES

LONDON

W11, of course. The Turbo likes W11 because everything is on the doorstep: cafés, restaurants, shops, friends. Most of her friends and contacts live here too. A scattering might also live in the more surprising parts of central London, the 're-thought' places where their grandparents and great-grandparents might have lived: Mayfair or St James. But most stick to W11. And they absolutely don't want to live amongst the basic Sloane.

NEW YORK

The West Village is the natural home of the Turbo. Not too far from Soho House and the comforts of the other Brits in New York in the Meatpacking District. If you're a slightly edgy Turbo, you may opt to live in the Meatpacking District itself.

TURBO STYLE

The Turbo Sloane is very fashion conscious but one simple rule applies to their taste: it's 'first-ist'. The Turbo adopts the very latest thing before anyone else does: a new Ferrari has just come off the line? The Turbo will have the first in London. It's a similar story with the new Mercedes – preferably a left-hand drive model to show that he's the continental sort. Otherwise he might drive a souped-up Range Rover equipped with all the latest satellite equipment. He will definitely have been among the first to have a NetJets card but he, of course, didn't pay the full price. He's big into gadgets (RSI from his Blackberry) and spends all his time online (on his Apple Mac Notebook) downloading iTunes (soft rock, Pink Floyd and Ibiza anthems from the previous summer); checking his Air Miles; emailing or scouring the internet for well-priced gadgets/private flights.

CLOTHES

The Turbo look: revived Savile Row suit, trainers and bigged up shirt. But here again, he always has to be first: the Turbo even pioneered MBTs

(Massai Barefoot Technology). When those strange platform shoes which promised to correct the posture landed in 2003, the Turbo wore them everywhere. The Turbo also loves Euro labels, often procured on shopping trips to New York; Polistas, the polo-players label, is currently a big favourite. And perhaps their leather gilet, too? And, of course, Vilebrequin for the beach.

TRAVEL

The Turbo is always abroad: weddings all over the world most weekends. He skis twice a year plus weekends (Verbier and Zermatt), flies to Mustique for Christmas and goes shooting in the Atlas. And he'll go anywhere other Turbos go: Argentina, Chile, St Tropez, Brazil, Ibiza, St Moritz, Mykonos, **Sardinia. And** of course, New York. He's incredibly hotel-savvy.

He's always in mid-air above the Atlantic. But when the Turbo thinks of where he'd *really* like to be his thoughts always turn to his childhood home and a gin and tonic on the terrace. Turbo's heart is in Gloucestershire.

The reality is it doesn't matter where Turbo is, Glos., New York, Paris, Dubai: he's terminally online, his BlackBerry's stuck to his palm.

EVENTS

The Hunt Ball no longer cuts it for this Turbo. He needs to be seen on the international circuit at the *Vanity Fair* Oscar party, at Elton John's Tantrums & Tiaras Birthday Ball, at the wedding in Colombia and at the hotter polo parties – specifically the three-day blitz in Argentina.

BONGO
SLOANE

Meet
Antonia

If Antonia Gunton was completely honest – and complete honesty is now Antonia's guiding principle – she wasn't happy throughout the twenty-three years of her marriage to Charles. Obviously she adored having the children. But the marriage? She wasn't happy. Not because of Lloyds, or the affairs, or even the rudimentary love-making. In fact it wasn't even Charles who made her so unhappy. It was herself. Antonia was not happy because she was not in touch with – nowhere near in fact – her *authentic* self. Never had been.

She can laugh now when she recalls that first diagnostic session with Sarah Peel. She hadn't seen Sarah since school, but then she bumped into her at the Hurlingham Club (looking utterly amazing) and Sarah told her she was now fully trained in feng shui. Feng what? Antonia had asked, imagining Sarah poised to offer some kind of kung fu-style attack.

The next thing she knew, Sarah had arrived at Rostrevor Road, which had not been decorated since 1986, and was counselling Antonia on the clash between fire and water created by her kitchen appliances. Sarah said that this was presenting 'major problems' in Antonia's life. How on earth did a kitchen function without fire and water? Antonia had asked, giggling into her glass of white.

But then she'd pulled herself together when Sarah, standing in their hallway, claimed that she could see money flowing straight out of the front door: Now that struck a chord. Charles had lost an awful lot of their money in Lloyds, and it was looking likely that they might not be able to keep Louisa at school.

Within twenty-four hours Antonia had installed
a three-legged toad facing the door which, Sarah had
counselled, 'suggested money coming in rather than
going out'. A week later she received a letter.

Antonia's Great Aunt Lavinia (who had shared
Antonia's passion for horses) had died, naming
Antonia the main beneficiary of her will. The
bequest included her house, Willow Cottage,
a paddock and stabling for six horses. Antonia
caught her breath and began to take feng
shui seriously.

In fact Lavinia's will marked the start of
Antonia's interest in a lot of foreign
sounding things. As Antonia's barefoot
guru says: 'You determine your state
according to the agreements you make
with yourself.' Learning that was one
of the hardest lessons of all: prior to
1994, and the start of Antonia's journey,
the only agreement that Antonia had
made was to marry Charles! Pre-1994 there
was no 'Me'. 'Me' just wasn't Antonia, or
her mother, or even Aunt Lavinia. It
certainly wasn't the Queen. English
people did not see things that way.

On Sarah's second visit she'd gone into the
bedroom Antonia shared with Charles: the trouble
with her nien yen and fu wei alignments turned out
to be no laughing matter. Antonia had already had her

first epiphany (she's had – and inspired – so many now she's lost count) and this time vigorously set about doing all that Sarah suggested.

At the time she and Charles had just celebrated their twenty-third wedding anniversary. The children were off doing their own thing – well, all of them except Louisa, who'd been a mistake and consequently was still at school – and Charles was approaching retirement. It had never occurred to Antonia to put herself first (the idea was excruciating), but she was beginning to see that doing so might be the way out of the rut she was in.

Over the next few months Antonia worked on the house and – she now realizes – herself. She re-aligned the dining room to ensure that all relationships were optimized by the place settings and she hung muslin, bamboo hoops and spherical crystals above the bed in an attempt to soften the atmosphere. It didn't work. Then Sarah suggested that the house contained too much blocked-up energy and that Antonia should see 'a wonderful man I know' who specialized in something called reiki. Six weeks and £600 later and at last Antonia felt she was getting somewhere.

The world and the angels, the healers and Antonia worked tirelessly to shift the blockage. Antonia started meditating at home and set up a shrine in a corner of the drawing room. Despite the fact that Louisa stole the crystals and the boys teased her about her whale music, Antonia felt lighter.

Charles failed to notice. Anything. He still poured her wine although she'd decided in January 1995 that alcohol was a poison (she's relented on that now and allows herself the occasional glass – for the antioxidants). He didn't seem to have registered that she no longer ate meat, or that she was no longer blonde. He did demand to know why his study now looked like 'a bloody conservatory' but Antonia didn't like to point out that they were money trees and he needed all the financial help he could get. He also resented their bedroom smelling like a 'ruddy brothel' with flowers festooned over every surface. It was the flowers that helped Antonia to make up her mind: freshly cut blooms – regardless of type – never survived more than two days in their bedroom.

Sarah agreed. Antonia and Charles were simply on different journeys. If Antonia had been living in her 'authentic self' in 1982 she would have seen then that their journeys were entirely incompatible and she would never have married him.

Divorce. The bombshell. It was terrible. Antonia was grateful her mother wasn't around to see it although Charles's mother more than made up for that by telephoning at all hours to point out the selfishness of it (she meant because of Lloyds), plus the fact that the boys were only just out of university and Louisa was fourteen. Fourteen! Antonia had clearly lost her mind.

Charles veered between bemused sympathy for his deranged wife, shock, and fury. His interpretation was simple: she'd gone mad. He began to poke amongst her herbal supplements to establish that she wasn't being drugged. He even talked to a chap at the club about symptoms of severe mental illness, but she didn't seem to fit the brief.

Charles failed to notice. Anything. He still poured her wine although she'd decided in January 1995 that alcohol was a poison.

It took all of Antonia's strength, yoga, meditation and almost daily visits to her reiki practitioner to get her through 1996. But to say it was worth it is an understatement. The old Antonia wouldn't recognize her life today.

Her new partner, Anzan ('Quiet Mountain'), is about a decade younger than her. They've been together for four years but Antonia is passionate that commitment is a choice you make every day not an institution you're enslaved to (she's learnt a whole new language) and their first encounter seems another lifetime ago.

The first time she met him was at her introductory Ayurvedic consultation. She was seeking advice about the knot of tension in her solar plexus that had persisted despite the fact that she'd left Charles several years earlier. Anzan overheard her

At fifty-eight, Antonia feels infinitely younger than that stiff young woman who, thirty-six years ago, shopped at Peter Jones, cooked shepherd's pie, wore navy tights and married Charles.

telling the consultant, 'I just want to say I have absolutely no faith in this at all', to which the consultant had replied that in that case, there was no point treating her. Anzan had stepped in with his generous smile and his warm eyes: 'Why not prove it to her?' Antonia had never seen anyone so incredibly beautiful – or fit.

Predictably, it was to be a life-changing session. As she left the clinic, Anzan held the door open for her and suggested they went for a coffee (a herbal tea as it turned out). Just a few months later they tried regulating their dosha energies and have been working together ever since. In fact Anzan has been a guiding light as well as a source of strength. The boys call him 'the Guru' and have largely accepted him – though recently George said that his mother should keep her money separate from Anzan's. This makes Antonia laugh – Anzan doesn't have any money to combine with hers. Even if he did, George needn't worry: Antonia isn't going to make that mistake twice!

The real change in Antonia's life has been Willow Cottage. The house left to her by Lavinia proved to be the means by which Antonia could finally and resolutely Obliterate Suffering With Bliss. Together, she and Anzan converted the stable block into a Yoga Retreat offering weekend breaks focusing on healing and meditation. They're already booked up for the whole of 2008.

At fifty-eight, Antonia feels infinitely younger than that stiff young woman who, thirty-six years ago, shopped at Peter Jones, cooked shepherd's pie, wore navy tights and married Charles. There's just no comparison. Thanks to yoga she's achieved things with Anzan she would previously have argued were physiologically impossible – not to say unnecessary. That's rebirth for you!

EVERYONE'S A LITTLE BIT BONGO

From the crucible of divorce rises the phoenix that is Bongo. Don't be fooled by the plumage: here again old Sloane values – and contacts – prevail.

She might be totally Bongo but she still looks forward to a glass of wine in the evening, cooks an excellent leg of roast lamb and will spend hours on the telephone to her girlfriends. Alongside these Sloane attributes are various additions: Bongo absolutely knows the right man for your bi-aura; the only place for your Ayurvedic colonic; and exactly how to position your money trees for maximum effect. She's become a confident source of cosmic advice.

The traditional Sloane view, that psychotherapy is something rather dangerous (and American!), is dying out with Bongo's mother. Bongo's ex-husband was also against it (see Thumping Sloane) but he's at least fifty miles away. Thank God.

With a lead from the Royal Family (even the Queen has tried reflexology; see also Prince Charles in Eco Sloane), Bongo has embraced all things alternative and at last has found something she's good at.

A coterie of healers and practitioners surrounds every Bongo, but as with everything in Sloanedom, none of these things should be taken too seriously or done too religiously. In short, most Sloanes these days are a little bit Bongo.

A STEP TOO FAR
Ashrams • Retreats • Vegetarians • Past-life regression
Channelling the dead

SLOANE AND HER CONTACTS

The Sloane is renowned for two things: her down-to-earth attitude to life (thanks to her upbringing) and her unsurpassed talent at forging and sharing useful contacts – 'I must give you the number for x, she's super at y; I absolutely swear by her!'

When it comes to Bongo, the normal Sloane contacts – a wonderful girl who makes curtains/dresses/necklaces in Battersea, say – have been superseded by contacts for crystal healers. And so in the past decade it has become apparent that Bongo's networking talent has outweighed generations of Sloane breeding. Indeed, through Parsons Green and Fulham Broadway, down into Putney, across to Balham and then back across the river to enclaves of Queens Park and W10, Bongo telephone lines twitter with the exchange of numbers for cranial osteopaths, iridologists, sacral healers, reflexologists and chakra clearers: 'You must go to this brilliant man. Completely got rid of Hugo's colic/ Martha's acne/ Jonathan's insomnia.'

Bongo can solve any one of her friends' and family's problems holistically through her support network of premium contacts. If the treatment is energy-based and the practitioner cheaper than others, Bongo is a Fan and the number – could be as far away as Southall – goes into her bulging Little Black Book.

DIANA, PRINCESS OF WALES

As usual when it concerns the New Sloane, Diana, Princess of Wales has a lot to answer for. There can be no doubt that Diana was the original Bongo Sloane. From 1981, when she married Prince Charles, she surrounded herself with a coterie of therapists. Most of what they did was completely unheard of (particularly amongst Sloanes). Even as recently as 1990, few were familiar with reflexology.

Ironically, Prince Charles (now leading the charge when it comes to all things Bongo) was 'appalled that his estranged wife and a member of the royal household would subject herself to this quackery'. How things change.

Diana persisted undaunted and throughout her life she consulted an impressive number of people, many of whom she fell out with and several of whom went on to write books about her. For several years she had twice-weekly sessions with Susie Orbach (psychotherapist and author of the 1973 tract *Fat is a Feminist Issue*) for help with her eating disorder. Rita Rogers was a favoured medium who foretold Diana's future. The energy healer and psychic Simone Simmons worked with the Princess for a number of years and, according to Diana's former butler Paul Burrell, would spend up to eight hours a day on the phone to her. Penny Thornton was employed as Diana's 'personal astrologer' and Dr Nish Joshi as her holistic detox guru. Oonagh Shanley-Toffolo (whom Diana met at the Hale Clinic, where she went for colonic irrigation) became her acupuncturist, later saying of the Princess that 'the whole landscape of her body was in total depletion'. Joseph Corvo was Diana's Zone therapist, taking care of the fifteen Zones on her face, Chryssie Fitzgerald was her reflexologist and Michael Skipwith her cranial osteopath.

THE SLOANE DIVORCE

Divorce came as something of a shock to the Sloane. She'd married at around the same period as Charles and Diana. And by the time they'd got divorced, Bongo was realizing that she too had had enough.

When Bongo got married, one's spouse was for life and so people – particularly women – just made do. Divorce was something only the grand, insane or battered went in for. Emotions were a distant memory – going off to school at seven years old had made sure of that – but reflexology, yoga and shrinks rather filled the void (until they became the route to epiphany). Perhaps life might be more fulfilling if one did even a little of what one wanted? Obviously the Queen wouldn't approve. But it's one thing ignoring emotions when you're the Queen and quite another when you're plain old Sloane.

When Sloanes first started getting divorces, sometime in the mid-1980s, things were much simpler. Bongo told Thumper she'd had enough and he did the

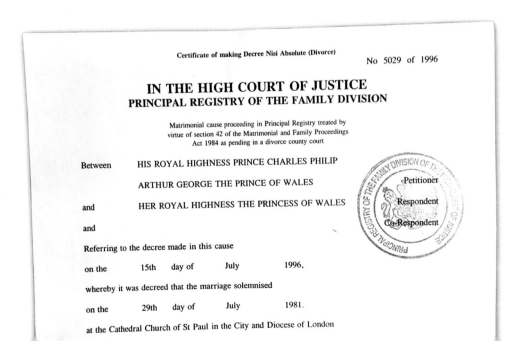

Certificate of making Decree Nisi Absolute (Divorce)   No 5029 of 1996

IN THE HIGH COURT OF JUSTICE
PRINCIPAL REGISTRY OF THE FAMILY DIVISION

Matrimonial cause proceeding in Principal Registry treated by virtue of section 42 of the Matrimonial and Family Proceedings Act 1984 as pending in a divorce county court

Between   HIS ROYAL HIGHNESS PRINCE CHARLES PHILIP

ARTHUR GEORGE THE PRINCE OF WALES   Petitioner

and   HER ROYAL HIGHNESS THE PRINCESS OF WALES   Respondent

and   Co-Respondent

Referring to the decree made in this cause

on the   15th   day of   July   1996,

whereby it was decreed that the marriage solemnised

on the   29th   day of   July   1981.

at the Cathedral Church of St Paul in the City and Diocese of London

honourable thing: he employed two solicitors – one for himself, one for his wife – gave Bongo and the children the house, paid her a good sum each month and moved into his mother's 'granny flat' a couple of miles up the road to lick his wounds.

Two things put paid to that: the Sloane got shafted by the Lloyds affair, so money was tight, and suddenly, now that there were Americans all over London and Brits in New York, American-style lawyer culture took hold.

The Sloane divorce, once a bastion of honour and discretion, turned nasty.

Prince Charles used Fiona Shackleton. A partner at Payne Hicks Beach, she has successfully negotiated the murky waters of separation for Prince Charles, Rick Stein and Paul McCartney and is now solicitor to William and Harry. Fiona (Benenden then Exeter) lives in Kensington and claims to own eighty-five scarves and a pair of shooting shoes. Herself a Sloane, she understands how awful these things can get. Discretion is everything.

Sloane divorce might be nasty but most Sloanes would still prefer to keep it low-key and cheap. Perhaps someone local? It doesn't always pan out that way though.

TAROT

The Sloane might have had her Tarot read for a giggle twenty years ago in the Romany Caravan at the village fête, but the idea of taking that kind of thing seriously was just not Sloane: it was too suggestible; too silly; too Bongo!

Today the Sloane faces testing times: marriage is no longer a certainty and it's certainly not for life; ascension to the first rung of the property ladder is not a given – Ma and Pa can't be counted on to help out; and nor are job offers automatic. Across the board the Sloane is having to compete in the open market. On top of that God can no longer be relied upon.

The potential pitfalls are endless and every Bongo needs a Tarot reader whom she can consult regularly. Most Bongos are fairly reticent about this. But the excellent Tristan Morell is recommended: not only does he have Romany blood, but he works in Notting Hill (and Brighton) and has helped more than one Bongo find their way.

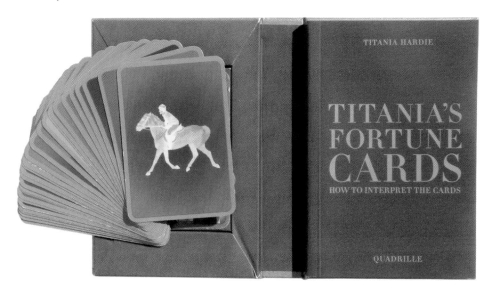

GHOSTBUSTERS

The trouble with Sloanes is that they like old houses. They like houses which have been in their family – or other people's – for generations. If a house is old it's likely to have the odd misplaced spirit wandering the corridors. Traditionally this has never been a problem: the Sloane is not the most tuned-in of beasts. But the arrival of Bongo, with her newly-opened chakras and raw, unleashed sensitivities, means that the old house plus its ghosts is now a nuisance which must be dealt with.

This is particularly the case when a Sloane family buys another's house. The resident ghost might not have minded rubbing up against the lives of kith and kin but a new family with a new Aga, a new Border terrier and new ways of storing outdoor clothing and logs… Some ghosts find such changes difficult to live with. This can cause problems.

Nicholas Coleridge and his wife Georgia had trouble with their country house in Oxfordshire, where a ghost was making a pest of itself by turning lights on and off. An exorcism by the nation's finest – Terry O'Sullivan – got rid of it and the Coleridges have lived in spirit-free bliss ever since.

Again, the Sloane who has had his house exorcized may be reluctant to own up for two reasons. Firstly, the Sloane is made of sterner stuff than to quake at a ghost. And secondly, the Sloane wouldn't want his friends thinking he had gone Bongo. As Nicholas replied when asked about the exorcism: 'Nothing to do with me… you'll have to ask my wife.' His wife, when asked, responded: 'He actually said that did he? It was me who was sceptical… and Nick who was spooked.'

YOGA

Yoga unites Bongos. The main thing about the Bongo path is that one's journey is one's own: while iridology may suit one Sloane, crystal healing will be the way ahead for another. Yoga however is the great Bongo bond. All Bongos do yoga (though confusingly, not all Sloanes who do yoga are Bongo). Yoga is an area in which Bongos right across the spectrum – from Carole Bamford to the Duchess of Cornwall to the Duchess of York to Sting and Trudie – feel comfortable. It's good for you in an uncontroversial way as well as being a First Step.

She'll most probably have been doing yoga for years, can do a headstand, attends two regular classes a week, and goes on Yoga holidays with a girlfriend every year, to Wales and Sri Lanka. That's what she spends money on, it's why she looks so good and its also why many Bongo Sloanes become yoga instructors. It's addictive.

Twenty-five years ago, only the cultish, the foreign or the sexually deviant did yoga; nowadays, along with Waitrose, a yoga centre is a fairly foolproof way of gauging just how Sloane a town, village or London postcode is.

ACUPUNCTURE

Acupuncture is an important part of Bongo's week and every Bongo will have a trusted acupuncturist who has become a friend and to whom she goes for her insomnia, her joints, her headaches and even her grey hairs. And she was doing it before Cherie. When Cherie's auriculotherapy – those needles in her ears – were all over the papers, Bongo did not come out to stand by Cherie and say that she also is a fan of pressure points. Bongo is one thing, aligning oneself with Cherie, quite another.

CATE MACKENZIE

All-round media guru Cate Mackenzie holds 'Open Your Heart' sessions by appointment at her office, conveniently situated close to Sloane Square. She teaches Sloanes to be receptive to all the nice things that might be coming their way. She also does customized heart paintings. Plus ultra-Bongo Internet radio.

CHANTING

Sloanes have come around to the benefits of chanting. Every Wednesday evening Cadoganshire hums with well-bred chants. Julia Stephenson – novelist (chalet-girl sagas), columnist for the *Independent*, Green Party candidate for Kensington and Chelsea, and member of the Vestey family – holds weekly sessions for Sloanes in her redbrick flat just behind Sloane Square. Sloanes scurry up to her and are invariably bowled over by the restorative effects of chanting 'Om!'.

LINSEED OIL

Bongo Sloane – along with the Duchess of Cornwall – has discovered linseed oil and has never looked back.

The first time she took it was rather disgusting and reminded her of the castor oil they gave her in hospital twenty-five years earlier when the baby wouldn't come out! But to know the benefits one only has to look at the Duchess of Cornwall's newly exquisite skin: she's said to have a flagon placed beside her plate at every meal. Bongo does the same. Her joints have never been so supple and her skin, hair and nails are as glossy as a new foal's. Her fridge is full of essential oils: walnut and linseed and Omegas 3 and 6. Lifesavers.

SLOANES SCURRY UP TO HER AND ARE INVARIABLY BOWLED OVER BY THE RESTORATIVE EFFECTS OF CHANTING 'OM!'.

THE WELL-KNOWN THUMPING SLOANE AND THE WELL-KNOWN SLOANE ACTRESS

A well-known Sloane was stunned when he arrived at an even better-known Sloane actress's North London house. Expecting drinks, he was astonished to be shown into a drawing room filled with the gently raised and the well-spoken who, looking flushed of face and sitting in a circle cross-legged on the floor, each clutched a pair of goat-skin drums on their laps.

As their excited hostess informed him, he'd arrived at a drum circle which was working to raise and heal energy and, perhaps most alarming, to release the spirits of the assembled. The beat started up as he was handed a pair of drums and our Sloane was invited to sit and join in when the rhythm beckoned him.

Appalled, our Thumping Sloane made his excuses and left. Ten years ago this stuff was largely unknown – except among those Trustafarian Sloanes who might have gone to India, done too many drugs and gone Off the Rails. Today it's perfectly acceptable for Bongo to take part in a weekly drumming circle. Her week wouldn't be the same without it. She's met so many people from so many corners of the world. And it's just so, well, primal somehow.

THE SLOANE THERAPIST

The Sloane steers clear of Harley Street. Plus all those other streets around there crammed with over-priced doctors. That's not to say that complementary therapist Dr Nish Joshi is over-priced but to the legendarily tight-fisted Sloane £75 for half an hour seems a little, well, steep.

Yes, Bongo will see therapists and healers and all the practitioners one would find on Harley Street, but Bongo would rather see them in the more obscure corners of London where they're at least half the price. And even if they're not, she just feels, well, better about it.

Hence her attitude to Nish Joshi. He might have been Diana's favourite alternative therapist for several years. He might have spent much time with her at Kensington Palace. But Bongo would still rather see a less well-known local practitioner than someone who is famous chiefly for the coterie of celebrities he attends to. In truth, Diana's stamp of approval is often enough to send Bongo seeking elsewhere.

PARTY
SLOANE

Meet
Jess

Jess, 30, used to be a fashion stylist and then Jamie Goodman, who runs all the clubs in London (all the ones worth going to) and with whom she's been friends for ever, asked her if she wanted to work with him. 'Doing what?'she'd laughed, shaking her hair off her face (unwashed for two nights – at least! She's hardly been back to her flat since, when was it, Friday?) as she sat at the bar in Red (one of Jamie's), wearing vintage Chanel – having knocked back probably her third or fourth White Hope cocktail – one Tuesday night in 2007. Honestly, after tonight, she'd already decided she was not going to drink for a month! They'd been watching the progress of a very pretty girl who, apparently, according to Aussie Rahul behind the bar, had pinched Shane Warne's butt on the dance floor and was just being escorted, shame-faced, to the door by two club staff. What the hell, Jess was wondering, was a sweaty cricketer doing in Red anyway? They really needed to re-examine their door policy.

Swiftly her eyes moved further down: those shoes. God in heaven! Wow! Just where did one go to get shoes like that these days?

'Oh, you know,' Jamie had explained, turning back to Jess as the girl was ejected and just as Prince William bowled in surrounded by his habitual posse of about ten or twelve. This group was immediately recognizable as clones of the Prince by their appalling clothes – did none of these people have any imagination? Predictably there were no women with them. Older MI5 officers, ever-vigilant and in badly fitting suits, looked about warily.

Jess watched over Jamie's shoulder as the heir to the throne stood for a moment in limbo between the bar and the door as staff – too cool to swarm over royalty – didn't rush over to show him to a table. And while Jamie downed another White Hope Jess allowed her mind to wander, what would she do if she were let loose on His Royal Highness? First off that sports jacket would have to go. It looked like the advert 'Man at Hackett'! And that shirt was really too much! It could have been one of his father's! God how sad! Her eyes travelled down: chino trousers – ugh, how gross was that? Swiftly her eyes moved further down: those shoes. God in heaven! Wow! Just where did one go to get shoes like that these days?

'I'm working on something you might be interested in,' Jamie had repeated.

Jess knew that what Jamie wanted was access to her address book. And why not? Half of London would kill for it. It was no secret that Jess had access to everyone and anyone and if she couldn't get them, chances were her flatmate Pete or one of her siblings certainly could.

Jess turned to Aussie Rahul. Ignoring the heaving clubbers clamouring to get drinks in front of her, Rahul served her immediately. 'Two White Hopes,' she said. The drink was so small – mostly vodka – that Jess knew the calories didn't matter and anyway,

like she'd said, she wasn't going to drink for a MONTH. She also wondered how anyone could survive if they actually had to pay for their drinks: these were almost a tenner a shot. A close friend of Prince William's rocked up; he appeared to be doing some kind of eratic robotics and was clearly out of his head. 'Jess babes,' he said, leaning forward to kiss her. He was sweaty as he fumbled to kiss her other cheek. Definitely another candidate for her styling advice. That bottle green velvet jacket would have to go. 'Seen Rose?' he asked, stumbling and looking unfocused beyond her.

She also wondered how anyone could survive if they actually had to pay for their drinks: these were almost a tenner a shot.

It was now that Jess heard the words 'New York'. She wiped the wastrel's sweat from her cheek and turned back to Jamie. 'I'd like you to help me set up a sister club in New York. We'd work on it together,' he was saying.

New York?

Her flat in Ladbroke Grove was sad now that Pete was in Arizona on that programme. And when he came out would things ever be the same again? Jack and Lou were in and out of the Priory the whole time, she hardly saw Jane now she was shacked up with Pierce and that baby etc. New York. Yes. Laurel and Amber were already in New York. Jackson was out there most of the time. It seemed the party had moved to New York. Why hadn't she realized that before?

'I want to call the new place Jessie's,' said Jamie, doing his Big Matey smile.

Jess smiled too. It would do her good, she decided, to divide her time between New York and London for a while. Time to make a few connections. Plus Jamie only ever went anywhere by private jet. And it wouldn't do her any harm at all to have Jamie Goodman's new club – in New York – named after her. No harm at all!

'You know everyone out there anyway,' continued Jamie. 'You know the Coles and Holly and Jay. Oh, and Rollo and Sara are out there now?' He counted the names off on his fingers. Jess sighed. Yes, she was at school with the twins, Rollo was always hitting on her and Sara was the daughter of her mother's school friend. And of course she had known Isaac and Sarah – she'd been invited to their Trailer Trash themed leaving party at Opium. She hadn't gone, why, she couldn't remember. Yes, she knew them all. She knew a lot of more interesting more glamorous party animals in New York too. Jamie was definately going to need her.

Aussie Rahul planted two vanilla-infused glasses on the bar in front of them. They drained the shots.

'I have to be here for June though,' said Jess placing her now empty glass back on the bar.

'It's Mathew Yearling's party.'

'Oh?' Jamie raised his eyebrows. 'NFI'ed.'

'Secret Summer at Yearling Hall somewhere in Suffolk. First year. He's doing a two-day micro festival. I'm helping him work out the guest list. You must come. I'll get you an invite.' Jess smiled as she said 'invite'. It made her mother apoplectic. However there were times – and this was one of them – when 'invitation' just didn't cut it!

'Do those things make money?' asked Jamie.

'Well,' said Jess, 'one thousand invites at 200 quid each. You do the maths. Plus everyone wants in on sponsorship.'

'Not bad for two days,' Jake nodded.

'If you've got a big house and a lot of land, it's certainly worth considering.'

She's cutting edge, she's cool, she's natty, she's super-funky *uber*-Sloane.

THE PARTY SLOANE: AN INTRODUCTION

Parties have always been as important to Sloanes as the Queen is to England: without them, the Sloane might cease to exist. The party is a way of reaffirming connections, of making new ones: a friend of a friend or even better, a leg-up with someone a Sloane would adore to be associated with – aristocracy, plutocracy, royalty, celebrity. These days, however, the party exists at its original level (a means of sharing like-minded conversation in order to reaffirm the boundaries between Sloane and non-Sloane) largely only outside London.

In London the Party has changed completely. It's now more, much more, than connecting over a glass. It's a way of life – a pretty lucrative one – for Sloanes on the make.

Parties in London are about a clique of Sloanes helping each other out. The Party Sloane is a 'doer': a club organizer, a back-scratching soul who spends time in Ibiza and has on speed dial the manager and frontman of every club and restaurant that counts. She's cutting edge, she's cool, she's natty, she's a super-funky *uber*-Sloane.

THE SEASON

It wasn't always this way: there used to be a Season which started in May with Queen Charlotte's ball – champagne, canapés and debutantes presented first to the Queen, and later to a cake – and ended with Glorious Goodwood at the end of August. Sandwiched between the two was an approved list of engagements which every Sloane should attend: the opening of the Summer Exhibition at the Royal Academy; Royal Ascot; Henley Regatta; Wimbledon; Chelsea Flower Show ; Cowes and what was left of the Victorian Season.

Nothing's the same nowadays: making drink-driving a criminal offence didn't help (gone are the days when the Sloane would drive back to Wiltshire after four bottles of champagne and a wonderful afternoon at Ascot); corporate boxes lent a distressingly commercial tone. But the Season had really died in 1958 (though Granny said 1939) when the Queen declared she'd had enough. It experienced a prolonged afterlife thanks to Mrs Kenward and Peter Townend who saw it through to the last Queen Charlotte's ball in 1994. In short, for the Sloane inside London, the Season as it was died. For the Sloane outside London, the Season has gone local (see Eco-Sloane). The Season died with The List. The List was buried with Peter Townend (1921–2001) and the Season with Mrs Kenward (Jennifer of 'Jennifer's Diary' 1906–2001).

MRS KENWARD 1906–2001

It's probably just as well that Betty Kenward is no longer with us: life was shocking enough in the 1990s without her having to deal with a relationship between an air hostess's daughter and the heir to the throne.

Mrs Kenward invented 'Jennifer's Diary' in 1944, when she went to work at *Tatler*. She wrote the column for the next forty-eight years (from 1959 for *Queen*, which became *Harpers & Queen* in the 1970s). 'Jennifer's Diary' remained unchanged for half a century and dwelt only on the Season and the private parties of the upper class. It read like the fussy notes of an demented matron. Mrs Kenward was once a Dame at Eton.

She prided herself on never speaking ill of anyone – which made for fairly challenging reading – except of course her sworn enemy Margaret, Duchess of Argyll, whom she blacklisted in 1963, by siding with the judge who presided over the Duchess's divorce, branding her 'immoral' and 'promiscuous'. She also maintained a feud with Peter Townend (see below), refusing to sit at the same table as him if they met at a party. But her most unfortunate sport was with Antony Armstrong-Jones. It began when AAJ was just a photographer on *Queen* and made the mistake of approaching her at a party. 'My photographers never speak to me at parties,' Mrs Kenward told him. A year later, he was Lord Snowden and engaged to Princess Margaret. On hearing the news, Mrs Kenward reportedly retired to her office where she repeatedly kicked her waste-paper basket, as she declared: 'What a turn up this is.'

Mrs Kenward always travelled first class on trains and insisted on a seat with her back to the engine, 'otherwise [it seemed she was oblivious to the end of the steam era] one gets so dirty'. Her telephone manner was brusque with those she considered her social inferiors. She was once interrupted 'as she hung sheets across the glass wall at *Queen* to avoid the sight of girls who,' she said, 'though top-drawer did not wash'.

Her look was inimitable: pearl choker, kid gloves and unmistakable champagne-coloured, crisp lacquered bouffant hair dressed with a trademark velvet bow which always matched her outfit. She would sail remorselessly through parties, tracking down important people. If there was no one of note at the two cocktail parties and one formal dinner she attended per night, she would say pointedly: 'Lovely party, unfortunately I did not know anyone at it.'

PETER TOWNEND, 1921–2001

Born in Leeds, Peter Townend suffered from meningitis as a boy and had very little formal education, both of which apparently contributed to the heroic powers of recall which helped him to compile The List each year.

His mother was an ardent fan of the aristocracy and the Royal Family and Peter grew up immersed in society magazines. He served in the Navy during the Second World War, and afterwards joined *Burke's Peerage*. It was while at *Burke's* that he metamorphosed from cheery Northern lad who lodged in a B.& B. in Beckenham to urbane stripe-shirted bachelor based in Chelsea unassailably intact. In 1968 he became Social Editor of *Tatler*, his task being to trawl the proofs of the Bystander pages correcting names and titles.

It was after the court presentation of debs ended in 1958 that Townend came into his own: he saw it as a personal challenge to keep 'the Season' alive. Thanks to his knowledge of and unrivalled obsession with the offspring of this nation's titled and landed, he succeeded in keeping its corpse twitching for the next forty years.

Townend incessantly combed the upper classes and serious plutocracy for girls approaching eighteen who might 'come out' the following year. To their mothers he sent elaborate turquoise letters. And so the Season became for Townend a never ending round of lunches, cocktail parties 'at home' and dances. The man existed entirely on canapés and champagne.

A stickler for punctuality, he hated last minute alterations: when a friend rang to cancel drinks because his grandmother had died, Townend responded, 'Oh. Oh. What am I to do this evening?'

And when, some time later, the friend joked about it, Townend apparently declared, 'Well, they don't bury people at night, do they?'

Townend materialized at every party where he would recite, in a stage whisper, the titles, connections and any gossip going into the photographer's ear. As the evening wore on, he would become increasingly lively. On the rare evening when there was no invitation, he would hit Claridges for champagne.

Towards the end of his life he lamented the national obsession with celebrity: 'It's a great shame that to be in the public eye a girl hasn't to be a top debutante or the fiancée of an aristocrat but must resort to such mundane acts as taking off her clothes.' He was sorry, too, that standards of hospitality had declined: 'There hasn't been a lavish party in England since the 1960s,' he declared shortly before he died.

He was one of the last men in England to deploy the epithet 'common' freely, however he was always chivalrous and when, some years ago, a girl ran naked through Queen Charlotte's Ball, it was Townend who wrapped her in a tablecloth and comforted her afterwards.

THE LAST OF THE DEBS
There is no argument with the fact that the Season proper died in 1958. As Princess Margaret famously declared: 'We had to put a stop to it. Every tart in London was getting in.'

In *The Last Curtsey: The Last of the Debutants*, Fiona MacCarthy, herself a 1958 debutante, offers an insight into those who were presented to the Queen that year. They included Sally Croker-Poole (married and divorced the Aga Khan); Nicolette Powell (left the Marquis of Londonderry for Georgie Fame); Teresa Hayter (joined the International Marxists); and Rose Dugdale, (became a 'freedom fighter' and joined the IRA). The Deb was dead.

THE NEW SEASON

Even before Mrs Kenward and Peter Townend croaked, the Sloane had wised up. Over the past decade and more the Sloane branched out from the Season's narrow confines into places where more fun was to be had: Glastonbury, Ibiza. In search of entertainment Sloanes found themselves in places which once might have been considered perhaps a little low-rent, more arty, borderline lefty. Meanwhile the reverse was happening with the traditional season: consider the car park at Royal Ascot these days, nose-to-bumper with white and pink stretch limousines.

There are ways and ways of doing Ibiza and Glastonbury and the way of the Sloane is not necessarily open to all Johnnies.

The Remains of the Season

While the traditional nineteenth-century Season lies in tatters, elements of it are still celebrated by the Sloane:

Point-to-points – huge!

Polo – huge! – especially the Chinawhite tent at Cartier!

Cowes – huge! – in yachting circles anyway.

Glorious Goodwood – everyone simply adores Lord March.

Henley Regatta – huge!

The Monaco Grand Prix – normally there is a ball but this year they're having a yacht instead – boo!

FESTIVALS AND CLUBS

GLASTONBURY

Glastonbury, for the Party Sloane, is rather last year. Trustafarians on the Portobello Road shake their dreadlocks as Notting Hill echoes with the cry: 'It's not what it was!' Criticisms range from 'too large' [read 'not exclusive enough'] to 'nowhere to pitch my tent' ['not exclusive enough'] to 'who wants to spend all day on the internet trying to get a ticket?' ['not exclusive enough']. The Sloane likes to know and be known or at least wants to be known by most of the people at a party.

If the Party Sloane is determined to do Glastonbury there are a couple of options worth considering: she should cause a stir by arriving in a helicopter (someone else's); she should buy (be given) a £1,500 VIP ticket with unlimited backstage access; she should go as a guest of the organizer or one of the bands, which should mean coverage of most of the above plus VIP accommodation complete with running water. Being a Party Sloane is about being singled out for something that little bit better.

THE MICRO FESTIVAL

It's much more fun and much more Sloane to be invited to an exclusive private festival hosted by a young blood in his own Stately, raising cash. Not only is the festival by invitation only, but on top of that each ticket costs several hundred pounds. These festivals are much cozier than Glastonbury, here everyone is already a friend or a friend of a friend or a friend waiting to be made.

KIMBERLEY HALL, IN NORFOLK

The granddaddy of the micro festival: the children are doing the heroic thing and saving the Big House for their beloved parents who still live there. Yes it's hired out for weddings and parties but it's the three day event in the summer that brings in the cash that keeps the crumbling pile upright. Invitations are notoriously exclusive and carry firm instructions: 'Do not tell the locals.' And a thousand Party Sloanes pile down from London to stay in luxury tepees and rage the nights away in the vaults

beneath the house and recuperate the days in healing tents having reiki, massage and reflexology. Rock on!

STANLEY HALL IN SHROPSHIRE

Hosted by Rollo Gabb and usually held on the last Bank Holiday in May. It's an extravaganza weekend of camel-racing, fire-eating and top DJs. As one of the hottest tickets of the summer, this party throngs with people considered by Sloanes to be 'way too cool' to be Sloanes. In short, this is a festival populated exclusively by the Party Sloane.

THE SECRET GARDEN PARTY

Hosted by the Hon. Freddie Fellowes (Eton, Newcastle) it's the perfect mini-Glastonbury just for Sloanes. On the vast de Ramsay estate on the Cambridge/Lincolnshire Borders, this festival delivers Pimms out of watering cans, a flamingo bar and bouncy castles. A space hopper Grand Prix and a pub quiz take place alongside DJs playing sets from tree houses. 'There was this crazy random metal detector in the middle of a field last year,' recalls one attendee. 'And there were all these wasted people queuing up to go through it!' Brilliant!

IBIZA

The only thing to do for August is to rent a house in Ibiza. Everyone's there in August. Easyjet or private jet, the Party Sloane, if not staying with the key Ibiza Sloane James Blunt, will rent a villa in Jesus or Ibiza Town, but never, never in San An

('Ugh! Really common!'). Everyone's there and days are spent on a boat on the turquoise waters at Formentera and nights at parties in each others' villas or at Pacha ('really cool!'). If work won't permit a month on the White Island, the Party Sloane will ensure she's at least out here for the all-important August Bank Holiday angling for a crucial invitation to James Blunt's cocktail party. If work is getting in the way of a month in Ibiza, why not make Ibiza work? (See Serena Cook in Turbo Sloane.)

CLUBS

In 1982 in London there were gents' clubs and a couple of Birley establishments. Twenty-five years on and the city's awash with private members' clubs set up by and partly for the Party Sloane. The pub is no longer where it's at. The Party Sloane is all about clubs. She loves to be a member of a club. She loves to be an initial member of that club (i.e. not pay) and she loves to be a member of a club where most of her acquaintances are also members – her richer, grander acquaintances anyway.

Clubs are formed with the Party Sloane – she who knows every clipboard girl and doorman in town – in mind. She can't remember the last time she paid for membership or for a drink but she is still valued at these establishments where she enjoys a status far higher than the Russian who spends £5,000 a night on champagne; above the Royal surrounded by secret agents and chums; and even above the Hollywood starlet whose posse occupies half the club and who has to be carried out, through the paparazzi, sometime the next morning. She's the local colour, the legitimizing 'real thing' that stops the place looking too trendy or too trashy.

TRACKING THE VIBE

The Party Sloane can track the vibe, thanks to her extensive network of cross-town contacts. Indeed her knowledge of what's happening on a given night in London is unrivalled and makes everyone else's efforts look distinctly amateurish: see P Diddy, London, March 2007: after dinner at Cecconi's in Mayfair, Diddy (plus entourage of six) went to Momo on Heddon Street. From there he went to private members' club Kemia for Snow Queen vodka martinis ('the vibe was wrong') and from there on to Maddox to dance. Unfortunately the vibe was 'all wrong' there too and so P, (plus entourage of twenty at this stage) upped and offed to Cristal where he took over an entire section of the club and necked a £30,000 bottle of Louis Roederer Cristal champagne to recover from his discomfiting evening. He obviously needed a Sloane Sherpa *that* night.

BOUJIS

Made famous by the Princes, the front man at Boujis is Jake Parkinson Smith, the Millfield-educated grandson of the great fashion photographer Norman Parkinson. The crowd is Sloane plus Euro Sloane, occasional film stars, frequent royalty and the odd footballer. The signature drink is the Crack Baby, a shot-sized mixture of vodka and champagne (£8). The Hackett-shirted (collars turned up) individual is likely to down several before livening up the dance floor (R & B and 'contemporary house' – nothing too challenging). If someone famous shows up, the Sloane will ignore them (acknowledgement could be uncool) unless of course they've met before (high fives; manly hugs; handshakes; champagne). The Princes are regulars. They show up quietly and drink steadily before being escorted out via the back entrance.

All is chilled in Boujis save for the occasional whoop of an Old Etonian having a fantastic time. The Notting Hill set arrive in their trainers and their skinny jeans; the Chelsea set in their nice dresses and nice shoes. The Euro set is the set to know here: they're the good-looking, well-groomed ones grooving on the dance floor with a bottle of champagne. The Russians might be vastly richer but they're generally best avoided – sitting as they will in dour groups in dark corners drinking Dom Perignon.

JESS DELIVERS HER VERDICT ON LONDON CLUBS

Chinawhite Wicked secret dining room!

Mahiki An excellent night!

Annabel's I love, love, love Annabel's! It's great fun. The bar men are sooo polite! Thursday is the night to go! Hope it stays the same sans Mark Birley!

Cuckoo Club Very Euro, very bling!

Amika Everyone's there on Thursday and Friday!

The Blue Bar Cool.

Notting Hill Arts Club Cool!

Hedges and Butler Good for a party.

151 Club Still really hilarious!

Kitts Fabulous cocktails!

Volsted Boujis's little sister. Very Euro.

Mo'vida Not a fan! It's full of unattractive guys!

Embassy Club (Mayfair) Incredibly naff!

Mamalanji Really lame! The club version of All Bar One!

THE WEST END

The Party Sloane feels iffy about the West End however Mahiki, (a) being at Green Park on the borders and (b) having a theme (Hawaiian – the Sloane loves a theme!) is a must. The Party Sloane has heard of other cool venues in other parts of London but will rarely go, it's still outside the known world.

A conversation (overheard) between Party Sloanes:
'I love the East End. But I never really go. It's much too far.'
'Hasn't Soho House opened in Shoreditch?'
'Oh yes, I think I heard that and what about Bistroteque? Doesn't it have fantastic cabaret nights?'
'Bistroteque? Isn't that somewhere in Hackney?'
'Is it? Oh God. Anyway there's that hotel somewhere over there if you can't make it back? The Z-something?'
'Oh yes, the Zetter.'

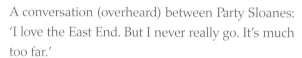

The Difficult Phase

At half term, school boys from Eton and Harrow in tracksuits are a familiar sight around King's Cross, Brick Lane, Brixton and Hoxton. At such times these places can resemble the Kings Road as they greet each other with cries of 'blud' and 'bruv' and by throwing up 'gang' signs.

This phase is nothing the Sloane parent should worry about. It's usually just a stop-gap between school and university, or just for one summer after university before securing the investment bank job.

THE PARTY SLOANE AND HER ADDRESS BOOK

The Sloane has realized that there are ways of cashing in on a good address book, which is why one should never throw out an old one, they might just make your living, and Smythson's age so nicely. Not only will a good address book make money, it will also up status and benefit everyone for miles around. Here's the key to a good address book:

If Ma and Pa were Sloanes and their parents before them and even their parents before them, the chances are that the Sloane, along with the children of their parents' friends and the grandchildren of their grandparents' friends, will all be Sloanes who are in some way connected. Perhaps their grandmothers were at Downe House together, or their fathers are Old Marlburians; the connection could even be as basic as that that *they* were at school together.

Equally perhaps they've met and re-met over the years on the beaches of Norfolk, Rock and Ibiza or on the Slopes of Verbier and Val d'Isère. A is B's cousin; C was the year below D at school; E's mother used to be married to F's father; G, H and I grew up in Northumberland next to J. And so on. And what better way to make use of one's connections than by carving out a very lucrative career in London. The Sloane is no longer shy about making money, and what better way to do it than by cashing in on a very obvious strength?

PARTY SLOANE CAREERS

1. Being hired as an Ambassador (touting for members) for an exclusive new club.

2. Setting up an exclusive new club.

3. Showing celebrities a good time in London at exclusive new clubs.

4. Organizing parties – often at exclusive new clubs.

THE SLOANE ORGANIZES PARTIES FOR OTHER SLOANES: CAPITAL VIP

Since the early 1980s there has been an incredibly lucrative market for instant teen Sloane parties created and cashed in on by various teen entrepreneurs. Eddie Davenport and Jeremy Taylor ran Gatecrasher throughout the 1980s, organizing parties and balls each school holiday at various London venues. School age Sloanes would descend on them to snog as many other Sloanes as possible.

In the 1990s teen entrepreneur Justin Etzin took up the baton and made a fortune running VIP Promotions. Capital VIP is now run by Will Bose. At £40 a ticket and more than a thousand guests at each party, how can they fail?

Today's party-goer is very different from his 1980s or even 1990s self when the whole thing was about drunken fumbling. These days, model-spotters are on hand to identify 'the look' amongst the *uber*-sophisticates on the dance floor in artful combinations of Top Shop and Chloé.

Party-goers today are as unlikely to be keeping score sheets as they are to be picked up at the end of the night red and sweaty in their parents' Volvos. These days they're collected by chauffeurs in Mercedes, their smart accents showing that it's cool to be smart, again.

'"Thank you, Capital VIP, for all your support and for buying my album in droves! I used to love these parties, see you all soon! James Blunt", 'reads the website. Along with:'"Congratulations Capital VIP, your party was extremely well organized, the teenagers had a great night," Royalty Protection Officer, Buckingham Palace, 2003.'

THE PARTY PLANNER

After the Sloane has left school however, she's usually less inclined to spend £40 on a ticket for a party in London where she'll be surrounded by thousands of (though still Sloane) strangers. In short, the market dries up after school. At this stage the Party Sloane will want to make parties work for her. She's so good at it, why not get paid for it?

And so the Sloane Party Planner will emerge, looking to make money.

What does the Party Sloane have that the billionaire doesn't? Contacts and a natural understated flair for throwing a party. The Sloane Party Planner is not a new thing:

LADY ELIZABETH ANSON

Lady Elizabeth Anson, a cousin of the Queen (once removed via Bowes-Lyons), set up Party Planners in 1960. She's organized, among other things, birthday parties for the Queen and Prince Charles, as well as parties for Tom Cruise, Mick Jagger and Donald Trump. She does the lot: food, flowers, music, lighting and invitations. Who wouldn't want the Queen's cousin in charge to ensure that all these things are ineffably right and un-naff?

Similarly Peregrine Armstrong-Jones (younger half brother of Lord Snowdon) has been putting himself out for years: he organized Posh and Beck's wedding as well as Zara's twenty-first.

Now that London is home to many of the richest people in the world, the Party Sloane has cottoned on to the fact that there's money to be made: the rich need someone to organize their parties. Elton John; Phillip Green, the department store boss, who spent £4 million on his son's bar mitzvah; P Diddy, who blew £175,000 on drinks at an impromptu party in London in 2007. Hedge fund managers keen to blow tens of thousands as an alternative route to a social life. The canny Party Sloane is planning parties for Russians and pop stars and Posh Spice.

QUINTESSENTIALLY

Many roads lead to Quintessentially, Ben Elliott's (the Duchess of Cornwall's nephew) global concierge service, which is the most sought-after Party Planner. 'They can get anyone from Beyoncé to Madonna,' or so the whisper goes. Past party triumphs include the Serpentine Gallery summer party (Mischa Barton, Elle MacPherson, Kristin Scott Thomas, Simon and Yasmin Le Bon); Diner des Tsars (Jemima Khan, Jaquetta Wheeler, Freddie Windsor); Jay Kay's birthday; *Vogue's* ninetieth; the Unicef dinner; and Hedgestock, yes, Hedgestock, the annual festival for hedge fund managers).

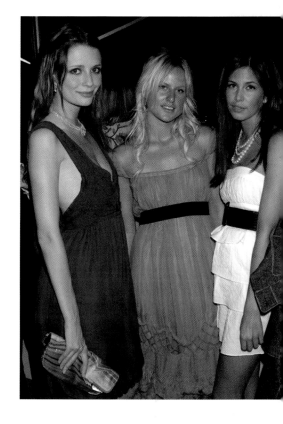

There are Sloane Party Planners making use of their contacts all over W10 and W11.

THE PARTY GOES CORPORATE

The contrast between those Sloane parties, (the modest *stand up and shout*) and today's Metropolitan Sloane party, (the quasi commercial party sponsored by a particular brand of liquor), exactly maps the shift in Sloane values. The Party Sloane has realized that it's all about commercial survival, which is about branding, getting things for free and not being ashamed to ask. Branding also demonstrates that you are considered important enough for these products to want to make the association. Plus of course, free alcohol! It's a no-brainer really: the less you pay, the better-off you remain.

The corporatization of the London party also marks the main difference between town and country. In the country, 1982 values are still current: what prevails there is, 'I bring mud in on my feet.'

THE SLOANE AND FANCY DRESS

Fancy dress has always been a big deal for the Sloane. The Sloane (still) loves to dress up. Why? It makes a party more fun. The Sloane will keep an extensive wardrobe including much fake Burberry and bling finds from Portobello Road. He is still mourning the tragic loss of Kensington Market. It was criminal to close it. They will also be on first-name terms with the staff at Angel's in Covent Garden. And will love, love, love Steinberg & Tolkien on the Kings Road!

A favourite theme, particularly in Edinburgh (where there's a Fancy Dress party at least once a week) is the Chav party: week in, week out, out come the Burberry, the Von Dutch and the gold belcher chains.

The key to Sloane fancy dress, particularly amongst the beautiful young is making oneself look unattractive: 'My favourite costume,' proclaims one beauty and Boujis regular, 'is a Loo! Bloody uncomfortable though!'

TOP THEMES

A & E • Chav • Trash • OAP • Evil Bastards • Bad Taste

Eugenie and Beatrice's efforts for Beatrice's eighteenth birthday party – a Victorian Ball to which they wore, along with their mother, sumptuous taffeta gowns – were largely considered uncool and unsuccessful: 'too try-hard!'; 'no self-mockery!'; 'took selves much too seriously!' (This last is considered a major failing by Sloanes.)

The Sloane particularly loves 'bad taste' fancy dress. Consider the Colonials and Natives party to which Prince Harry wore that Nazi uniform and after which he received such a pasting. 'Not a big deal at all!' recalls one attendee. 'You should have seen some of the other costumes!' He goes on to recall another fancy-dress party he attended shortly after 9/11: 'Someone came as the Twin Towers!'

PUBS IN LONDON

Sloanes of a certain age are often extremely batey about the fact that most of the old Sloane favourites have been converted into private houses or shops. This includes at least ten on the Kings Road and, more importantly, the Phene Arms (a combination of George Best and roaring Sloanes kept old residents awake for decades). The Moore Arms on Moore Street also mourned (now two houses) as well as the Australian on Milner Street (once a celebrated spot for ra's to meet over foaming pints), and perhaps most distressing of all, the Shuckborough (now a boutique bakery) which was once celebrated all over London as the spot where a famous Sloane, at the end of each working week, would order two bottles of champagne: with one he would spray his colleagues and with the other he would toast his accuracy. They might be batey but when it comes down to it the brutal truth is that these places are no longer Sloane locals. The Sloane has not been local to these areas for at least a decade: ousted by Euros, Yanks and Russians, most Sloanes can't afford to live in these pockets around Sloane Square. Unfortunately for the publicans in these parts, Euros, Yanks and Russians don't as a rule patronize their friendly local, either.

The Sloane map of London has changed radically in twenty-five years and the Sloane local can now be found in areas where the New Sloane lives: Clapham; Wandsworth; Balham; North Kensington and Queens Park.

The countryside is also studded with Sloane pit stops. There's something about Metropolitan Sloanes: they'll go out of their way – sometimes by hundreds of miles – to be together. In Gloucestershire it's the Hare and Hounds in Westonbirt; the Vine Tree at Randwick; the Cat and Custard Pot at Shipton Moyne and the Tunnel House in Coates. In Edinburgh they might favour the Wally Dug on Northumberland Street, the Cumberland Bar on Cumberland Street or Iglu on Jamaica Street.

In Cornwall they'll convene in Rock at the Mariners, in Polzeath at the Oyster Catcher. In East Sussex it'll be the Griffin Inn in Fletching; in Wiltshire, the Lamb in Hindon; in Oxfordshire, The Village Pub in Barnsley; in Dorset, the Museum Inn near Blandford Forum; in North Yorkshire, the Star Inn outside Helmsley. Last but not least in Norfolk they will gather at the Victoria in Holkham and the Hoste Arms in Burnham Market.

No other social group has such a comprehensive and wide-spread network of established places to drink.

The Rural Sloane is a different creature: he'll go to a good local, talk to anyone (not just fellow Sloanes who are likely to be in short supply) and make friends with the landlord.

THERE ARE STILL SOME 'DESTINATION' SLOANE PUBS THRIVING IN LONDON

The Anglesea Arms in Selwood Terrace

The Admiral Codrington in Mossop Street

The White Horse in Parsons Green

The Ladbroke Arms off Ladbroke Grove

The Builders Arms in Chelsea

The Duke of Wellington (The Duke of Boots) in Eaton Terrace

The Crown in Dovehouse Street

The Pig's Ear in Old Church Street

The Hollywood Arms in Hollywood Road

Aragon House in the New Kings Road

The Windsor Castle in Campden Hill Road

The Ship in Wandsworth Bridge Road

The Westbourne in Westbourne Park Villas

The Cow in Westbourne Park Villas

SLOANE DATING

Despite the layers of Sloane connections, and the network of mostly Sloane pubs and members' clubs, dating isn't necessarily easier in Sloane-land. In fact, Jess and most of the people she knows are still single. Internet dating just isn't really Sloane: it smacks too much of Sloane off the Rails. The Dinner Party's practically vanished (it was designed around Sloane singles meeting other singles). So when it comes to the Sloane and dating, there was rather a gap in the market. It took a canny Sloane to plug it.

THE SUPPER CLUB

Tamsin Lonsdale: 'When I set up the club it was about me and my friends. I was twenty-seven and a lot of my friends were dabbling with speed dating and internet dating. I thought despite everything being so social it was really difficult to meet people so I set something up for People Like Us. It's difficult for Sloanes to meet other Sloanes as everything is quite cliquey and what the Supper Club does is introduce you to friends of friends.'

Who is Tamsin Lonsdale? Educated at Bedales, Daddy was at Sherbourne before making stacks of money with Jean Machine. Her official biography is to the point: 'From an early age Tamsin was mingling with families from the Astors to the Simons, who remain close friends to this day, it reads. 'She was always determined to make her own fortune though and so after school she embarked on a business degree at Edinburgh University.'

All this has certainly stood her in good stead and the Supper Club currently has 1,000 members with 500 on the waiting list. It's expanding to New York and Tamsin is adamant that her success is down to the fact that she 'won't compromise quality over quantity:

every fortnight we meet 100 prospective members at one of our cocktail parties and we take 17 per cent. I'm looking for attractive people with personalities. I want the actress, I want the entrepreneur, I want the It-Girl. I want the celebrity. It's that which makes for an exciting dinner'.

Membership costs £150 a year (each event is charged on top) and for that you get the 'opportunity to get into places you might not otherwise be able to; Chinawhite, Adam Street, the Electric, Soho House'. And of course you meet a lot of Sloanes too.

WEEKEND HOUSE PARTIES

The weekend house party has changed. No longer does it run from Friday night to Sunday night; it now begins on Saturday either just in time for lunch or just in time for supper and is over shortly after lunch on Sunday. Just 24 hours. It's better for both the host and the guest: the host doesn't want his house turned upside-down for three days, and the guest, with only two days respite, may very well not want to spend them both in the country, missing things.

These days guest and host are both working much harder than they were in 1982. As one Sloane points out: 'there's no such thing as a Sloane playboy these days, they're all working much too hard. Even Freddie Windsor (son of Prince and Princess Michael of Kent, thirtieth in line for the throne and one-time resident of Kensington Palace) has had to get a day job!' Having dabbled in film – it just wasn't paying the bills – Freddie found work with American bank JP Morgan at the end of 2006.

BLENHEIM ESTATE

There are house parties on one particular estate to which every Sloane would love an invitation; indeed they'd probably not even insist on arriving late on Saturday afternoon and leaving early on Sunday morning. It's the place where the occupants (and there are several households here) compete to have the most impressive guest down to stay – Hollywood, Political, Literary. The various households get together for drinks or supper to display the calibre of their own house-guest. One stunned Sloane recalls: 'x had one of the big Hollywood actors down; y had Seinfeld down; z had someone even better down. Unbelievable!'

Blenheim is a combination of grand-house-and-family plus big-name-London-media heavies. Richard Curtis and Emma Freud have a house here, as do Matthew Freud and Elisabeth Murdoch; *uber*-hacks Rebekah Wade and Simon Kelner also have houses in Blenheim (though not together) and so too does sandwich plutocrat, Julian Metcalfe.

THE DINNER PARTY

The Dinner Party is not what it was. No longer do girls in flats in Earls Court spend Thursday night giggling away as they struggle to whisk the lumps from their white sauce to finish the lasagne before they wrap it in cling film, shove it in the fridge and bring it out again, amid candles and slightly plastered, mostly single guests, on Friday nights.

Something along these lines (though with better thought out food!) might exist mid-week in the Nappy Valley Sloane colonies of Wandsworth, Balham and Clapham – the lawyer belt. Something along similar lines may very well still exist at the weekend in the country, but in London things have certainly changed.

Completely new kinds of dinner party are happening in London Party Sloane-land.

THE DAVID CAMERON KITCHEN SUPS

In most London houses, particularly in W10, the basement dining room is all part of the kitchen. No triple tripod regency table decked with silver candlesticks.

Here, owners will host a power supper mid-week, where power workish things are discussed: media, politics. Everyone will know at least one front bench member and one broadsheet editor.

Guests will be casually dressed, food (both parties work) will be good and shop-bought (a pie from

Lidgate's or organic beef – on the bone – from the same and either those 'Gu' puddings from Waitrose or a fruit tart from a nearby patisserie for pudding). The dinner will be all about the conversation; it's miles cooler and more eclectic.

THE BANKING PARTY SLOANE'S DINNER PARTY
The Banking Party Sloane, aged 30 to 40, gives an altogether different dinner party. It will be held on a Thursday, Saturday or Sunday evening and these dinners are not really about food at all which, incidentally, will be conservative, excellent, very expensive, cooked by a silent woman in the kitchen and served by a silent butler (both will have been brought in for the night).

The evening will revolve around cocaine ('c'caine') and the filet of beef, vegetables and white chocolate mousse will go largely untouched. After dinner there'll be more c'caine and then the whole party will reconvene at Boujis.

SPLIT THE BILL
Owing to work commitments (exhaustion) and the fact that most Sloanes don't have large enough London spaces to hold dinner parties these days, the Sloane is much more likely to go out to dinner with friends at London restaurants and split the bill. Not the old bread roll throwing, Tim-nice-but-dim Sloanes, but the sleek, chic Party Sloane instead.

'Split the Bill' perennials include the Electric; Crazy Homies; the Cow; Essenza; Kensington Place ('always a classic!') and E & O in Notting Hill. Then there's Carpaccio in Sydney Street; Brinkley's on Hollywood Road ('It's an institution! John Brinkley is a *legend*!'); Eight over Eight in Chelsea; and of course that old Sloane favourite, La Famiglia in Langton Street. Foxtrot Oscar (will it survive being Ramsay-fied? Probably not).

The rules are as follows: no matter what's been had (starter, no starter) the bill will be split evenly (unless of course someone just turned up for a glass of wine). No quibbling, no bill checking, no missing wallets.

DRUGS

The Party Sloane won't always say no to drugs and weekend cocaine is still around. And, appealing to the daft Sloane streak, there's still that dinner party thing of passing around a canister of nitrogen oxide (laughing gas) available from Mr Whippy and all other suppliers for ice-cream vans. The Party Sloane is not deterred by strong language ('All other use other than for ice-cream is illegal') or threats,('…will result in prosecution.')

At the festivals drugs are central, now including cocaine, MDMA, marijuana and liquid acid. Yes, liquid acid. The Sloane at the festival goes mad for liquid acid, sometimes literally (see Sloane Off the Rails).

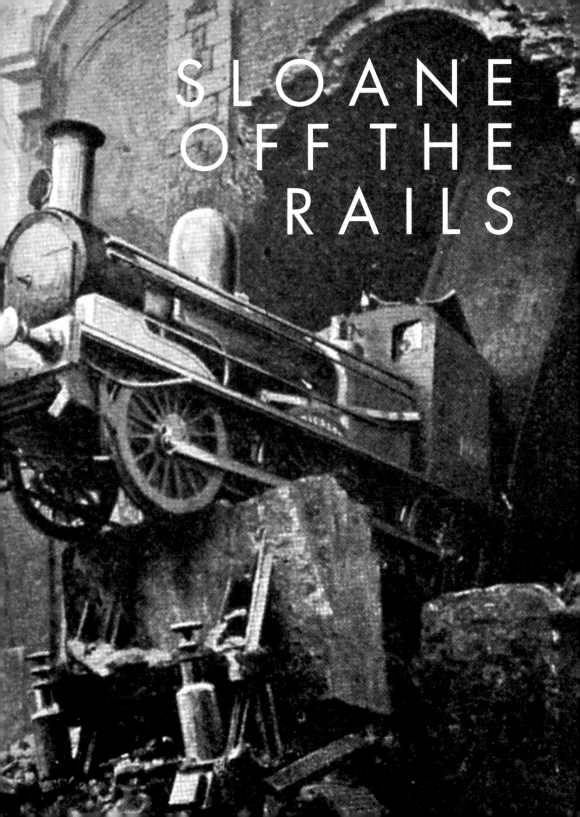

SLOANE
OFF THE
RAILS

Meet
SJ

Sarah Jane (SJ): twenty-six; Benenden; Marlborough (for A levels – her parents thought it would do her good to meet a few boys); St Andrews (English 2:1) and now Condé Nast where she's features editor on one of their magazines – one of the youngest ever – and is doing glitteringly well. She was recently headhunted by a 'family' newspaper but, to the immense relief of her parents, she chose to stay in Hanover Square – they had to almost double her salary to keep her. Although they both read that newspaper ('I know it's rubbish,' Sylvia, SJ's mother, giggles, 'but it's wonderful rubbish, isn't it?') neither relished the idea of having a hard-boiled hack for a daughter. No, Condé Nast suits her just fine: gentle, clever and exquisitely beautiful – friends are always suggesting that she should be a model.

With her glossy hair and her coltish elegance she's just like her mother when she was that age.

With her glossy hair and her coltish elegance she's just like her mother when she was that age.

SJ has never been short of admirers. In fact her parents – Sylvia in particular – had nursed high hopes that she'd marry a particular Marquis she'd met at St Andrews. Things had been going so well that SJ had brought him down to Hampshire prompting Sylvia to have the curtains in the drawing-room cleaned (for the first time in a decade!) and also get the girls in from the village to give The Grange a going-over. Jonathan had retreated to the conservatory, muttering about what he called the 'Royal Visit'. That weekend, while Jonathan stood on the terrace with the boy, she gave SJ a swift refresher on 'the Rules', particularly the importance of not sleeping with him too soon.

'Mummy,' SJ had groaned. 'We're only friends.' But Sylvia could tell. When she and Jonathan were alone, she asked whether he thought the boy's parents would share the bill.

'What bill?' Jonathan had asked. 'For the wedding, darling, SJ's wedding.'

Jonathan, who was uncertain if anyone was good enough for SJ – his own little sausage – had allowed the thought to cross his mind. Not the thought that the Marquis of Thingy would pay up for his boy – Jonathan knew damned well that he wouldn't – but the thought of 600 guests and a lifetime's penury.

Sylvia was completely untroubled. She heard his name mentioned now and then, even after SJ left St Andrews and began sharing a flat in Putney. It was during one of these telephone conversations about eighteen months ago that SJ had said: 'Mummy, I've started doing the Alpha Course'.

'Oh, have you darling?' Sylvia had asked vaguely. Her mind was elsewhere, she was wondering if there was any way she could avoid having to cancel the bridge four on Thursday evening because of Jonathan's shooting.

'It's about forging a closer relationship with Jesus,' SJ had said. 'It's about letting the Holy Spirit into your heart. It's about discovering why we're here.'

'Sounds lovely, darling,' her mother had replied. Religion was something Sylvia approved of; she had always enjoyed a good relationship with God, going to church at least once a month – it didn't look good if their pew was empty for too many weeks on the trot – and it was good to catch up with the village. And so she forgot all about it.

And then her daughter came home breathless with excitement one Saturday lunchtime and kept going on and on about a weekend she'd spent – somewhere outside Morecombe – on her knees, speaking in tongues, with tears rolling down her cheeks. 'Mummy, I felt the Holy Spirit enter me.'

Sylvia was not quite sure how to take this: it seemed that her beautiful daughter had not only found God but had dropped everything else for Him, which just might amount to a problem.

'Oh, let her!' Jonathan had said. 'The girl's happy, isn't she?'

SJ certainly seemed happy but that was hardly the point.

'She'll grow out of it,' Jonathan had suggested.

'Mummy, I felt the Holy Spirit enter me.'

Eighteen months later and SJ was showing no signs of growing out of it. If anything, she was even more involved in the whole thing: she was at HTB (Holy Trinity Brompton) most nights of the week handing out leaflets, running groups and helping in the kitchen.

Sylvia watched her dream of SJ becoming a Marchioness recede as SJ handed in her notice on the flat in Putney and moved into a place in Earls Court – 'I can walk to the church!' – with a friend she had met at HTB, of course.

When Sylvia had been her age there hadn't been a single man in London who hadn't wanted to take her out. Now SJ was wasting her best years inside some fusty church as part of the Born-Again God Squad.

'Oh, Mummy, it's not like that! You should come. I think you'd love it.'

And so Sylvia had come down on the train and had taken a taxi from Waterloo to the church in Knightsbridge. It had been crowded, though the people weren't as socially drab as she'd feared. But she just couldn't bear to see that open-hearted, wholesome relationship with God: all of them sitting in groups, breathlessly discussing their experiences with Jesus Christ and holding hands to pray. Group prayer, group experience: all that touchy-feely stuff. It was just too enthusiastic. Sylvia knew that prayer was like an account: you paid in, privately, and only God knew your balance. A more traditional kind of God and Church was something to be visited once a fortnight. Sylvia knew what to do: it was time to withdraw from her account. 'Dear God,' she prayed that night, 'please make SJ leave that dreadful church, and find her way back to the Marquis.'

THE SLOANE OFF THE RAILS

While the Sloane has taken on board a mass of New Age thoughts and styles of behaviour in the past twenty-five years, there are still some bridges too far. But there are some too who have gone over entirely and have ended up cast out by their community into a world beyond the frontiers of Sloaneland. Their mistake? To harbour any view, opinion or addiction which takes over one's life, allowing no room for the natural rhythms of Sloane.

A return from the hinterland can be made although more by luck than design. Consider, for example, the Eco Sloane: the Prince of Wales; Tracy, Marchioness of Worcester; and anyone else who, ten years ago, refused plastic bags in supermarkets. Just a decade ago they were considered crackpots, barefoot whackeroos. Thanks, however, to the cyclical nature of things and the fact that climate change has come

Essential Sloane Attributes

- not taking oneself too seriously – boring!
- not being too earnest – boring!
- not having rabid beliefs – boring! Unless, of course, they are to do with hunting, farmers or New Labour
- not spending too much time banging on about 'me' – boring!
- having the ability to tell a good – i.e. scurrilous, scandalous and potentially life-wrecking – story at dinner
- ability to laugh at self
- self-deprecation

ECO SLOANES, FORMERLY OFF THE RAILS, BROUGHT IN FROM THE COLD TO BE RE-LODGED IN THE SLOANE BOSOM:

The Prince of Wales
Tracy, Marchioness of Worcester
Zac Goldsmith
George Monbiot
Hugh Fearnley-Whittingstall

into Sloane focus and has even been taken to the Sloane heart (see Eco Sloane), the former nuts are now firmly inside the Sloane tent – more, they've become gurus. Think Hugh Fearnley-Whittingstall: the man eats road kill and human placenta. Ten years ago the average Sloane would have recommended that F-W was sectioned; today, he's a hero.

Currently Green is good but Sloanes can still slide off the rails.

Other paths once leading to Sloane Off the Rails, now firmly back in the Sloane fold:

- environmental freak (see Eco)

- yoga fanatic (see Sleek)

- money-obsessed (see Turbo)

- buddhist (see Bongo)

- obsessed with grooming (see Sleek)

SARAH FERGUSON

The Duchess of York was Sloane. A more basic
model than Diana and more typically Sloane.
Sadly for Sloane, Sarah went badly Off the Rails.
If she was looking for a route back now, the
outlook – at this point, anyway – would
not be good.

She began life as the daughter of Major
Ronald Ferguson ('the galloping Major' –
Eton, Sandhurst, then polo manager first to
the Duke of Edinburgh and later to the Prince
of Wales). Her mother bolted with an
Argentine polo player when Sarah was just
twelve years old, leaving her in Hampshire
on Dummer Down Farm, her childhood
home. She grew up with one of the best
seats in Pony Club camp.

After school she went to secretarial college
before getting a job in PR in London. She
then worked in an art gallery followed by a
publishing house and before long she was going
out with Prince Andrew – thanks to the machinations
of her great friend Diana, Princess of Wales. They were
married in 1986 and the following year the Duchess
of York became the first woman in the Royal Family
to get her pilot's licence.

So far, so Sloane!

By 1992, she and her husband had drifted apart and Sarah was spotted with other men, mostly Americans. First it was Texan oil baron Steve Wyatt and then, more memorably, she was photographed – topless – having her toe sucked by one John Bryan. This was not good. Her divorce came through in 1996, by which time Sarah had been ostracized by the Royal Family and cast out by the press who called her the 'Duchess of Pork' and 'Frumpy Fergie'. She was also damned by Sir Martin Charteris, former private secretary to the Queen, who exclaimed that the duchess was 'vulgar, vulgar, vulgar' (he's since denied it). Finally it emerged that she'd run up debts of £4 million living her extravagant life.

It wasn't just that which blasted Fergie from Sloaneland. Rather it was her own re-creation to which Sloane objected and, in particular, the fact that in the process she sold herself – and her Duchesshood – to America. On top of her £1 million annual salary as US ambassador to Weight Watchers, she wrote self-help books including *Reinventing Yourself with The Duchess of York*. She's designed a range of home

fragrances for the American market and is in big demand as a motivational speaker on the after-dinner circuit over there, for which she bares all regarding the royal marriage, her subsequent vilification in the press, her spectacular demise and her triumphant resurrection. Making money from Yanks is fine, but doing it in public with psychobabble, that's too much.

Perhaps her most blatant venture was a foray into advertising: the voice of Sarah Ferguson tells the story of a beautiful young girl swept off her feet by a knight on a white charger who whisks her off to a fairytale castle. The camera then cuts to Sarah in the flesh: 'Of course, if it doesn't work out, you'll need to understand the difference between a P/E ratio and a dividend yield, a growth versus a value strategy.'

So here we've got Weight Watchers, home fragrances, self-help books, capitalization on a failed marriage and too much candour. It's not really very Sloane.

As for the Royal Family, it's not surprising that they felt it had to come to some kind of agreement with Sarah to guarantee that she would never tout her wares on this side of the pond. What was shocking was that Sarah just couldn't be trusted to know how to behave!

'Poor Fergie!' Sloanes sigh.

'Ghastly!' others chorus.

THE ABOMINABLE GINGE

James Hewitt is another Sloane who went irredeemably Off the Rails. Transgressions of honour like his are not easy to fix, indeed they put you beyond the pale, probably for ever. Adultery is fine, as long as it is carried out in the appropriate way. Hewitt? Unforgivable.

His early life was Thumping: Millfield, then Sandhurst followed by a career in the Cavalry in the first Gulf War. Hewitt was even mentioned in dispatches in 1991.

Then it was back to Blighty where he became riding instructor to the Princess of Wales and from there to the bedroom – for at least five years. As Diana said in that Panorama interview, 'Yes, I adored him. Yes, I was in love with him. But I was very let down.'

It was not just Diana, Princess of Wales, who was let down when James Hewitt co-operated with Anna Pasternak on *Princess in Love*, the book which charted their affair. As if that wasn't enough, Hewitt's own biography *Love and War*, published in 1999, offered a still more explicit account of the relationship. And just two years after the Princess's death, he was on both sides of the Atlantic touting – for £10 million – his love letters from the Princess. The word 'cad' was revised just for him. On top of that, Sloane always had trouble taking seriously a man who emerged from the loins of a woman called Shirley.

CAMILLA, DUCHESS OF CORNWALL

By rights Camilla should be a Sloane Off the Rails. In 1970 when she was Prince Charles' girlfriend, she was judged not to be wife material by the Royal Family. In 1973 she married Andrew Parker Bowles, an Army officer and a friend of the Prince.

Not good enough for the Royal Family raises questions for Sloanes. On top of that came the recordings of that telephone conversation with Prince Charles in which he said he wanted to be her 'Tampax'. A bit too close to Fergie's toe-sucking if you ask Sloane.

But thanks to Camilla's indomitable sense of humour, her smoking, her hunting and her ability to secure the heart of the heir for almost four decades, she has been given the thumbs-up by most Sloanes, even though the Queen and the Duke of Edinburgh didn't attend the civil ceremony celebrating their marriage in 2005. This, together with the dignity with which she has handled everything else thrown at her, make her a woman from whom any Sloane on the brink could learn huge lessons.

CAMILLA'S LESSONS

- Don't bare the soul
- Don't go candid on prime time TV (with or without Martin Bashir)
- Don't go public
- Don't apologize
- Don't explain

- Don't kiss-and-tell
- Don't do self-help stuff
- Wear a good hat
- Get back in the saddle
- Look as though one has more important things to worry about than the way one looks

SLOANES ON THE VERGE

There are always masses of Sloanes who are almost going Off the Rails. Curiously, Prince Harry is not one of them. Despite the fact that Harry, third in line to the throne, has behaved in various ways unbefitting of royalty – taking drugs, lashing out at photographers, calling the French chef at the pub on his father's Highgrove estate 'a fucking frog' and, as widely reported, telling barmaids in Canada that his name is Gary in order to fondle them incognito – they are conventional Naughty Boy transgressions, all fine at his age. The bottom line is that he is not a Marxist, a vegetarian, a Jehovah's Witness or anti the War in Iraq. Bravo Harry!

SLOANES IN DANGER

Lady Victoria Hervey pretty far gone (too tacky)

Dave Cameron getting too earnest

Zac Goldsmith ditto

POLITICALLY OFF THE RAILS

Being seriously political is a surefire way to be cast out of Sloanedom fast. 'Political' means having more than strong opinions, i.e. not of the Dave Cameron variety which are, of course, entirely Sloane.

It is particularly un-Sloane to head left. Anything even remotely suggestive of the redistribution of wealth is completely unacceptable: a return from the far left is at best unlikely and is usually impossible.

WEDGIE BENN

Born in 1925, the second Viscount Stansgate was elected Labour MP for Bristol South-East in 1951. Following this he spent twelve years pushing through the Peerage Act of 1963 which allowed the renunciation of peerages. He went on to become the first peer to renounce his title and having done that he moved on to other things. He spent much of the 1970s attempting to get details of his education – Westminster, New College, Oxford (President of the Oxford Union) – removed from *Who's Who*. In 1973 he took things even further when he announced that he wanted to be known simply as Mr Tony Benn rather than his original name, Anthony Wedgwood-Benn. (Wedgwood as in the Staffordshire pottery.)

A vegetarian since the 1970s, a highlight of Benn's career came when in 1965 he proposed issuing stamps without the Queen's head on them. The Queen herself stepped in to stop the republican measures. He was also a public supporter of Sinn Fein. Inevitably one thing led to another and by 1991 he'd proposed the abolition of the monarchy.

The Sloane verdict on Mr Tony Benn? Cracked.

TONY BLAIR

Tony Blair is a Sloane Off the Rails but a much more insidious and dangerous kind than Wedgie Benn. At least Wedgie presented himself as cracked from the outset: there were no nasty surprises there.

Blair is a different story. In 1997 he looked like your average, modern Sloane: Fettes (the Eton of the north), Oxford and then the Bar. Yes, he was head of the Labour Party, but it was a *New* Labour which fitted the Sloane notion of treating the working classes with compassion (as long as nothing infringed on the Sloane's own life). Why not improve state education, improve the NHS and help single mums? thought genial Sloane.

Mrs B might have been Liverpudlian but hadn't they met at the Bar? Of course Cherie would know broadly how to behave. A few Sloanes voted for Blair only to conclude that their PM was a weak man entirely in the thrall of his socialist wife with New Age habits.

He went utterly Off the Rails and sold his own kind down the river in order to stay in power so Sloane thinks. He attacked all that was most dear to the Sloane – hunting, smoking and farming – and turned this once-great nation into an authoritarian police state. Traitor.

The Sloane does not do Traitors! For Sloanes, Tony Blair was the most unpopular prime minister in a century. The bottom line is, was he a True Sloane or just First Generation masquerading as Sloane?

MARXISM

Marxism was a phase which the old Sloane just might have gone through if he'd got in with the wrong crowd at the wrong university. The hope is that it is just that, a phase brought on by a temporary lapse of judgement or temporary alignment with an unsuitable friend.

All the same, it's safest to steer young Sloanes away from dangerous establishments which have the potential to bend tender ears.

DANGEROUS UNIVERSITIES

Liverpool • UEA (the University of East Anglia) • SOAS LSE • Aberdeen • Leeds • Warwick

TARA PALMER-TOMKINSON

Tara Palmer-Tomkinson has crossed several lines. First she was ostracized by the royal family then for several years her behaviour leaned towards the 'erratic'; finally there was that extraordinary appearance on the Frank Skinner show and admission of a £400 per day cocaine addiction. She was whisked off to Arizona to deal with it.

Back in London her rehabilitation was completed with numerous appearances on Reality Television and satellite TV channels.

Despite the transgressions, Tara is not entirely, irredeemably, Off the Rails. Why not? Why do Sloanes still respond to Tara? What does she have that Sarah Ferguson doesn't? The ability to laugh at herself: a self-deprecating sense of humour. Even if your nose has collapsed entirely, as Tara's did in 2006, it's important to keep on trucking – she's got that engaging have-a-go style!

As any Sloane would say: 'I'd never do what she has done, but at least she's open and honest and can laugh at herself.'

REHAB

The Sloane in rehab is a new
thing. It used to be that Sloanes
dried out occasionally at
Champneys (or a similar 'health
farm'). Lots of Sloanes drank
rather a lot but that was about it.

By the 1990s came addiction,
much soul-searching and a choice
of rehabilitation clinics.

In the beginning Sloanes went to the Priory to 'deal with' anything that was
making them 'boring!'. The Priory is now no longer the only clinic of choice: in fact,
despite its reputation for being a lot of fun, it is also slated among some Sloanes
for having a high-return ratio for patients. The Priory might be a good way to meet
celebrities but it's more important to get rehab right. (After all, rehab's not cheap
and it costs anything from £15,000 to £60,000 for a four- to six-week programme.)

WARNING SIGNS THAT A SLOANE COULD BE HEADING OFF THE RAILS

- Volunteers at the local church
- Starts going door to door – collecting/proselytizing for anything, except of
  course the Conservative Party in one's own village
- Stops eating meat
- Starts meditating and talking about things like the New Consciousness, One's
  Higher Self, the coming Age of Aquarius and Eradicating the Memory of
  Troublesome Past Lives
- Gets rid of car, citing Global Warming

CLINICS OF CHOICE

Promises (Malibu): a good option for the Sloane interested in Hollywood celebrities.

Cottonwood (Arizona): complete lack of luxury, fabled for its 'pureness' and popular with Sloane parents.

The Meadows (Arizona): a 12-step programme plus rigorous timetable including dawn rise followed by t'ai chi, mediation and prayers.

Promis (South Kensington and Kent): very popular with the Sloane; good London address plus high success rates, though initially difficult for Sloanes as it's focused on 'discussing feelings'.

The Causeway (Osea, Essex): popular with the Turbo Sloane, as it's just twenty minutes by helicopter from London. Plus very good food: the chef from the Ebury now cooks here. Very luxurious. Very expensive.

Capio Nightingale (Lisson Grove): no frills, no nonsense, no Church. Popular with Sloanes who have already failed elsewhere.

Farm Place: addiction-focused sister hospital to the Priory. Not as nice as it sounds.

Clouds: this is a charity so it costs less than half as much as other clinics for a six-week stay. Good value (v. Sloane).

DIRECTORY

ECO

Abel & Cole
08452 626 262
www.abel-cole.co.uk

Anya Hindmarch
15-17 Pont Street, London SW1X 9EH
020 7838 9177
www.anyahindmarch.com

Baby List
The Broomhouse, 50 Sulivan Road
London SW6 3DX
020 7371 5145
www.babylist.co.uk

British Wind Energy Association
Renewable Energy House, 1 Aztec Row
Berners Road, London N1 0PW
020 7689 1960
www.bwea.com

Bryn Parry Studios
14 Parkers Close, Downton Industrial Estate
Downton, Wiltshire SP5 3RB
01725 513 212
www.brynparrystudios.com

C K Press
148 Sloane Street, London SW1X 9B
020 7730 0975
www.ckpress.com

Candle Shop
50 New Kings Road, London SW6 4LS
020 7736 0740
www.candlesontheweb.co.uk

Certified Farmers' Markets
0845 45 88 420
www.farmersmarkets.net

Connaught Square Squirrel Hunt
www.csshhq.org.uk

Countryside Alliance
The Old Town Hall, 367 Kennington Road,
London SE11 4PT
020 7840 9200
www.countryside-alliance.org.uk

Cranborne Stores
1 The Square, Cranborne, Dorset BH21 5PR
01725 517 210
www.cranbornestores.co.uk

Daylesford Organic
Daylesford, Nr. Kingham, Glos. GL56 0YG
01608 731 700
www.daylesfordorganic.com

Duchy of Cornwall
Station Road, Liskeard
Cornwall PL14 4EE
01579 346 473
www.duchyofcornwallholidaycottages.co.uk

Duchy Originals
The Old Ryde House, 393 Richmond Road,
East Twickenham TW1 2EF
020 8831 6800
www.duchyoriginals.com

Earth Natural Foods
020 7482 2211
www.earthnaturalfoods.co.uk

The Ecologist
102 D Lana House Studios,
116-118 Commercial Street, London E1 6NF
020 7422 8100
www.theecologist.org

The Field
9th Floor, Blue Fin Building,
110 Southwark Street, London SE1 0SU
www.thefield.co.uk

G Wiz
GoinGreen, Green Station
201 Beaconsfield Road, Middlesex UB1 1DA
020 8574 3232
www.goingreen.co.uk

Hunter wellies
Hunter Boot Ltd., Edinburgh Road, Heathhall,
Dumfries DG1 1QA7
01387 269591
www.wellie-boots.com

James Jeans
www.jamesjeans.us

Kaftans Direct
1 Villa Road, Bingley, West Yorks BD16 4ER
01274 566 247
www.kaftans-direct.co.uk

Kaftans for girls
Pink Bamboo, 25 Herndon Road
Wandsworth, London SW18 2DQ
020 8874 8660
www.pinkbamboo.com

Kazzbar
020 8941 8651
www.kazzbar.co.uk

Lazy Environmentalist
0845 337 2015
www.lazye.co.uk

Lidgate's
110 Holland Park Avenue, London W11 4UA
020 7727 8243

London Allotments
www.londonallotments.net

London Farmers' Markets
11 O'Donnell Court, Brunswick Centre
London WC1N 1NY
020 7833 0338
www.lfm.org.uk

Maroque
01449 723 133
www.maroque.co.uk

Mutton Renaissance Club
10-12 Picton Street, Bristol BS6 5QA
0870 242 3219
www.muttonrenaissance.org.uk

Neal's Yard
15 Neal's Yard, London WC2H 9DP
020 7379 7222
www.nealsyardremedies.com

Organic Pharmacy
396 Kings Road, London SW10 0LN
020 7351 2232
www.theorganicpharmacy.com

People Tree
1st Floor, 91-93 Great Eastern Street
London EC2A 3HZ
020 7739 9659
www.peopletree.co.uk

Pure Incense
www.pure-incense.com

Save Sloane Square
27 Walpole Street,
London SW3 4QS
020 7730 2800
www.savesloanesquare.co.uk

Sequoien CIC
91 Bere Lane, Glastonbury
Somerset BA6 8BE
01458 833 256
www.sequoien.com

Terre d'Oc
184 Kings Road, London SW3 5XP
020 7349 8291
www.terredoc.com

CHAV

Barbour
0191 427 4210
www.barbour.com

Bliss
60 Sloane Avenue, London SW3 3DD
020 7590 6146
www.blisslondon.co.uk

Blue Bar
The Berkeley Hotel, Wilton Place
London SW1X 7RL
020 7235 6000
www.theberkeleyhotellondon.com

Boujis
43 Thurloe Street, London SW7 2LQ
020 7584 2000
www.boujis.com

Burberry
21-23 New Bond Street
London W1S 2RE
020 7968 0000
www.burberry.com

Butlins
0870 242 1999
www.butlinsonline.co.uk

Center Parcs
0870 067 3030
www.centerparcs.co.uk

Chanel
167-170 Sloane Street
London SW1X 9QF
020 7235 6631
www.chanel.com

Chinawhite
6 Air Street, London W1B 5AA
0871 075 1734
www.chinawhite.com

Christian Dior
30-31 Sloane Street, London SW1X 9NE
020 7235 1357
www.dior.com

Christian Lacroix
80 Sloane Street, London SW1X 9LE
0171 235 2400
www.christian-lacroix.fr

Christian Louboutin
23 Motcomb Street, London SW1X 8LB
020 7245 6510
www.christianlouboutin.fr

Cobden Club
170 Kensal Road, London W10 5BN
020 8960 4222
www.cobdenclub.co.uk

The Collection
264 Brompton Road, London SW3 2AS
0871 075 1397

D & G
175 Sloane Street, London SW1X 9QG
020 7201 0980
www.dolcegabbana.it

Daphne's
112 Draycott Avenue, London SW3 3AE
020 7589 4257
www.daphnes-restaurant.co.uk

E & O
14 Blenheim Crescent, London W11 1NN
020 7229 5454

French Sole
6 Ellis Street, London SW1X 9AL
020 7730 3771
www.frenchsole.co.uk

Funky Buddha
15 Berkeley Street, London W1J 8DY
020 7495 2596
www.fblondon.co.uk

Goat in Boots
333 Fulham Road, London SW10 9QL
020 7352 1384

Hari's
305 Brompton Road, London SW3 2DY
020 7581 5211
www.harissalon.com

Harvey Nichols
109-125 Knightsbridge, London SW1X 7RJ
020 7235 5000
www.harveynichols.com

Hollywood Arms
45 Hollywood Road, London SW10 9HX
020 7349 7840
www.hollywoodarms.co.uk

Holmes Place
188a Fulham Road, London SW10 9PN
020 7352 9452

Jimmy Choo
32 Sloane Street, London SW1X 9NR
020 7823 1051
www.jimmychoo.com

Joe's Cafe
126 Draycott Avenue, London SW3 3AH
020 7225 2217
www.joseph.co.uk/joes.htm

Joseph
74 Sloane Avenue, London SW3 3DZ
020 7591 0808
www.joseph.co.uk

Juicy Couture
www.juicycouture.com

Julie's
135 Portland Road, London W11 4LW
020 7229 8331
www.juliesrestaurant.com

Mamalanji
107 Kings Road, London SW3 4PA
020 7351 5521

Manolo Blahnik
49-51 Old Church Street
London SW3 5BS
020 7352 8622
www.manoloblahnik.com

Mazda
www.mazda.co.uk

Personalised number plates
www.personallyyours.co.uk

Prada
43-45 Sloane Street, Knightsbridge, London
SW1X 9LU
020 7235 0008
www.prada.com

Ragdale Hall Health Hydro
Ragdale Village, Melton Mowbray,
Leicestershire LE14 3PB
01664 434 831
www.ragdalehall.com

Ray-Ban
www.ray-ban.com

Roberto Cavalli
181-182 Sloane Street, London SW1X 9QP
020 7823 1879
www.robertocavalli.net

Tunnel House
Tarlton Road, Coates, Glos. GL7 6PW
01285 770 280
www.tunnelhouse.com

Ungaro
150 New Bond Street, London W1S 2HD
0207 629 0480
www.ungaro.com

Versace
183-4 Sloane Street
London SW1
020 7259 5700
www.versace.com

Wagamama
www.wagamama.com

White Horse
1-3 Parson's Green, London SW6 4UL
020 7736 2115
www.whitehorsesw6.com

Zuma
5 Raphael Street, London SW7 1DL
020 7584 1010
www.zumarestaurant.com

THUMPING

Boden
0845 677 5000
www.boden.co.uk

Boodle's
28 St James Street, London SW1A 1HJ
020 7930 7166
www.boodles.org

Brook's
60 St. James's Street, London SW1A 1LN
020 7493 4411

Country Sports
www.countrysports.co.uk

Countryside Alliance
The Old Town Hall
367 Kennington Road, London SE11 4PT
www.countryside-alliance.org.uk

Finca Buenvino
Los Marines, 21208 Huelva, SPAIN
+34 959 124 034
www.fincabuenvino.com

Foxtrot Oscar
79 Royal Hospital Road, London SW3 4HN
020 7352 7179

Hackett
137-138 Sloane Street, London SW1X 9AY
020 7730 3331
www.hackett.com

Harvie & Hudson
96-97 Jermyn Street, London SW1Y 6JE
020 7839 3578
www.harvieandhudson.com

La Famiglia

7 Langton Street, London SW10 0JL

020 7351 0761

www.lafamiglia.co.uk

La Poule au Pot

231 Ebury Street, London SW1W 8UT

020 7730 7763

Ladbroke Arms

54 Ladbroke Road, London W11 3NW

020 7727 6648

New & Lingwood

53 Jermyn Street, London SW1Y 6LX

020 7493 9621

www.newandlingwood.co.uk

St. Moritz Cresta Run

www.cresta-run.com

Support Hunting

www.supportfoxhunting.co.uk

Swinton Park

Masham, Ripon, North Yorks HG4 4JH

01765 680 900

www.swintonpark.com

T. M. Lewin

103-108 Jermyn Street, London SW1Y 6EQ

020 7839 3372

www.tmlewin.co.uk

Turnbull & Asser

71-72 Jermyn Street, London SW1Y 6PF

020 7808 3000

www.turnbullandasser.co.uk

Turf Club

5 Carlton House Terrace, London SW1Y 5AQ

020 7930 8555

SLEEK AND EURO

Annabel's

44 Berkeley Square, London W1J 5AR

020 7629 1096

Aubaine

260-262 Brompton Road, London SW3 2AS

020 7052 0100

www.aubaine.co.uk

Baker and Spice

54-56 Elizabeth Street, London SW1W 9PB

020 7730 3033

www.bakerandspice.com

The Basil Street Practice
3 Basil Street, London SW3 1AU
020 7235 6642
www.basilstreetpractice.co.uk

Bluebird
350 King's Road, London SW3 5UU
020 7559 1000

The Brompton Cross Clinic
13 Crescent Place, London SW3 2EA
020 7052 0070
www.bxclinic.co.uk

Capital VIP
www.capitalvip.com

Collection
264 Brompton Road, London SW3 2AS
020 7225 1212
www.the-collection.co.uk

ColourNation
53 Endell Street, Covent Garden
London WC2H 9AJ
020 7836 8883
www.colournation.com

Cowshed
119 Portland Road, London W11 4LN
020 7078 1944
www.cowshedclarendoncross.com

The Cuckoo Club
Swallow Street, London W1B 4EZ
020 7287 4300
www.thecuckooclub.com

Dr. Mosaraf Ali at
The Integrated Medical Centre
43 New Cavendish Street
London W1G 9TH
020 7224 5111
www.integratedmed.co.uk

Eclipse
113 Walton Street, London SW3 2HP
020 7581 0123
www.eclipse-ventures.com

Eight Over Eight
392 Kings Road, London SW3 5UZ
020 7349 9934

Elistano
25-27 Elystan Street, London SW3 3NT
020 7584 5248
www.elistano.com

Fere Parangi at Neville's
5 Pont Street, London SW1X 9EJ
020 7235 3654

Feroza at Colour Nation
53 Endell Street, London WC2H 9AJ
020 7836 8883
www.colournation.com

Gucci
18 Sloane Street, London SW1X 9NE
020 7235 6707
www.gucci.com

Harbour Club
Watermeadow Lane, London SW6 2RR
020 7371 7700
www.harbourclub.co.uk

Hermès
179 Sloane Street, London SW1X 9QP
020 7823 1014
www.hermes.com

Hurlingham Club
Ranelagh Gardens, London SW6 3PR
020 7736 8411
www.hurlinghamclub.org.uk

Ivy
1-5 West Street, London WC2H 9NQ
020 7836 4751
www.the-ivy.com

**Jean-Louis Sebagh at The French
Medical Cosmetic Company**
25 Wimpole Street, London W1G 8GP
020 7637 0548

Jeroboams
50-52 Elizabeth Street, London SW1W 9PB
020 7730 8108
www.jeroboams.co.uk

Jo Hansford
19 Mount Street, London W1K 2RN
020 7495 7774
www.johansford.com

Josh Wood at Real Hair
6-8 Cale Street, London SW3 3QU
020 7589 0877
www.realhair.co.uk

Julia Biddlecombe
www.juliabiddlecombe.co.uk

KX
151 Draycott Avenue, London SW3 3AL
020 7584 5333
www.kxgym.co.uk

Lambton Place Health Club
Westbourne Grove, London W11 2SH
020 7229 2291
www.lambton.co.uk

The Life Centre
15 Edge Street, London W8 7PN
020 7221 4602
www.thelifecentre.com

Louise Galvin at Daniel Galvin
58-60 George Street, London W1U 7ET
020 7486 9661
www.danielgalvin.com

Lucio
257 Fulham Road, London SW3 6HY
020 7823 3007
www.luciorestaurant.com

Movida
8-9 Argyll Street, London W1F 7TF
020 7734 5776
www.movida-club.com

Nicholas Lowe at Cranley Clinic
19a Cavendish Square, London W1
020 7499 3223

Nikita's
65 Ifield Road, London SW10 9AU
020 7352 6326
www.nikitasrestaurant.com

Oliveto
49 Elizabeth Street, London SW1W 9PP
020 7730 0074

Philip Treacy
69 Elizabeth Street,
London SW1W 9PJ
020 7824 8787

PJ's Restaurant and Bar
52 Fulham Road, London SW3 6HH
020 7581 0025

Poilane
46 Elizabeth Street, London SW1W 9PA
020 7808 4910
www.poilane.fr

Polistas
12-13 Burlington Arcade
London W1J 0PH
020 7495 6603
www.polistas.com

Princess Nails
131 Walham Green Court,
London SW6 2DG
020 7385 9288

Queens Club
Palliser Road, London W14 9EQ
020 7385 3421
www.queensclub.com

Robin Oakey at Footopia
Peter Jones, Sloane Square
London SW1W 8EL
020 7259 0845
www.peterjones.co.uk

Robinson Valentine
4 Hornton Place, London W8 4LZ
020 7937 2900

San Lorenzo
22 Beauchamp Place, London SW3 1NH
020 7584 1074

Sophie at The Berkeley
Wilton Place, London SW1X 7RL
020 7235 6000
www.the-berkeley.co.uk

Strip
112 Talbot Road, London W11 1JR
020 7727 2754
www.2strip.com

Third Space
13 Sherwood Street, London W1F 7BR
020 7439 6333
www.thethirdspace.com

Tim Bean at Total Physique Management
305 Bluewater House, Smugglers Way
London SW18 1EB
020 8870 4557
www.totalphysiquemanagement.com

Tramp
40 Jermyn Street, London SW1Y 6DN
0870 201 4837

Trevor Blount Pilates
5 Harrington Road, London SW7 3ES
020 7584 0680
www.trevorblountpilates.com

Vaghela Kamini at Kamini Salon
14-16 Lancer Square, London W8 4EP
020 7937 2411

Vaishaly Patel at Vaishaly Salon
51 Paddington Street, London W1U 4HR
020 7224 6088

Volstead
9 Swallow Street, London W1R 7HD
020 7287 1919
www.volstead.com

TURBO

The Admiral Codrington
17 Mossop Street, London SW3 2LY
020 7581 0005
www.theadmiralcodrington.co.uk

All Star Lanes
Victoria House, Bloomsbury Place
London WC1B 4DA
020 7025 2676
www.allstarlanes.co.uk

Annabel's
44 Berkeley Sq, London W1J 5AR
020 7629 1096

Aragon House
247 New Kings Road, London SW6 4XG
020 7731 7313
www.aragonhouse.net

Beatrice Inn
285 W. 12th Street, NY NY 10014
+1 212 243 4626

Belu
0870 240 6121
www.belu.org

Boden
0845 677 5000
www.boden.co.uk

Boujis
43 Thurloe Street, London SW7 2LQ
020 7584 2000
www.boujis.com

The Box
189 Chrystie Street, NY NY 10002
+1 212 982 9301

The Builders Arms
13 Britten Street, London SW3 3TY
020 7349 9040
www.geronimo-inns.co.uk/thebuildersarms/

The Builders Arms
1 Kensington Court Place, London W8 5BJ
020 7795 4811

Bungalow 8
515 W. 27th St, NY NY 10011
+1 212 629 3333

Cate Mackenzie
www.catemackenzie.com

The Chocolate Bar
48 Eighth Avenue, NY NY 10014
+1 212 366 1541
www.chocolatebarnyc.com

Cipriani Rainbow Room
30 Rockefeller Plaza
NY NY 10112
+1 212 632 5000
www.cipriani.com

The Cuckoo Club
Swallow Street, London W1B 4EZ
020 7287 4300
www.thecuckooclub.com

Cumberland Bar
3 Cumberland Street, Edinburgh EH3 6RT
0131 558 3134
www.cumberlandbar.co.uk

Deliverance
0844 477 1111
www.deliverance.co.uk

The Electric
Electric House, 191 Portobello Road
London W11 2ED
020 7908 9696
www.the-electric.co.uk

Eos
Eos Airlines
0808 234 8759
www.eosairlines.com

Glasses Direct
0845 688 2020
www.glassesdirect.co.uk

Hotel on Rivington
107 Rivington Street, NY NY 10002
+1 212 475 2600
www.hotelonrivington.com

Iglu
2B Jamaica Street, Edinburgh EH3 6HH
0131 476 5333
www.theiglu.com

Kittichai
60 Thompson Street, NY NY 10012
+1 212 219 2000
www.kittichairestaurant.com

La Esquina
203 Lafayette Street, NY NY 10012
+1 646 613 7100

Luxury Publishing
www.luxurypublishing.co.uk

Macelleria

48 Gansevoort St, NY NY 10014

+1 212 741 2555

www.macelleriarestaurant.com

MAXjet

0800 023 4300

www.maxjet.com

Netjets

020 7361 9620

www.netjets.com

Nobu

19 Old Park Lane, London W1K 1LB

020 7447 4747

www.noburestaurants.com

Oka

60 Sloane Avenue, London SW3 3DD

020 7590 9895

www.okadirect.com

Pastis

9 Ninth Avenue, NY NY 10014

+1 212 929 4844

www.pastisny.com

Payne Hicks Beach

10 New Square, Lincoln's Inn

London WC2A 3QG

www.paynehicksbeach.co.uk

Quintessentially

www.quintessentially.com

Rolex

191 St. James's Square, London SW1Y 4JE

020 7024 7300

www.rolex.com

The Rose Bar at Gramercy

2 Lexington Avenue, NY NY 10010

+1 212 920 3300

www.gramercyparkhotel.com

Silverjet

0844 855 0111

www.flysilverjet.com

Soho House

29-35 Ninth Avenue, NY NY 10014

+1 212 627 9800

www.sohohouseny.com

The Spotted Pig

314 W. 11th Street, NY NY 10014

+1 212 620 0393

www.thespottedpig.com

The Tunnel House

Tarlton Road, Coates, nr. Cirencester

Glos. GL7 6PW

01285 770 280

www.tunnelhouse.com

Vilebrequin
56 Fulham Road, London SW36 6HH
020 7589 8445
www.vilebrequin.com

The Waverly Inn
16 Bank Street, NY NY 10014
+1 212 243 7900

The White Company
8 Symons St, London SW3 2TJ
0870 900 9555
www.thewhitecompany.com

White Cube
48 Hoxton Square, London N1 6PB
020 7930 5373
www.whitecube.com

BONGO

Ali Norell
07802 589 630
www.heelyoursole.co.uk

Alpha Courses
Holy Trinity Brompton,
Brompton Road, London SW7 1JA
0845 644 7544
www.alpha.org

Anya Hindmarch
15-17 Pont Street, London SW1X 9EH
020 7838 9177
www.anyahindmarch.com

British Association of Psychotherapists
37 Mapesbury Road, London NW2 4HJ
020 8452 9823
www.bap-psychotherapy.org

College of Cranial-Sacral Therapy
9 St George's Mews, London NW1 8XE
020 7483 0120
www.ccst.co.uk

Dr. Mosaraf Ali
The Integrated Medical Centre,
43 New Cavendish Street, London W1G 9TH
020 7224 5111
www.drali.com

Dr. Nish Joshi
57 Wimpole Street, London W1G 8YW
020 7487 5456
www.thejoshiclinic.com

Dr. Robert Svoboda
www.drsvoboda.com

Eden Medical Centre
63a Kings Road, London SW3 4NT
020 7881 5800
www.edenmedicalcentre.com

Find a drum circle
www.drumcircle.meetup.com

Float
2a Bridstow Place, London W2 5AE
020 7727 2133
www.float.co.uk

Graham Roos
07772 089 347
www.grahamroos.com

Guild of Naturopathic Iridologists
94 Grosvenor Road, London SW1V 3LF
020 7821 0255
www.gni-international.org

Life Centre
15 Edge Street, London W8 7PN
020 7221 4602
www.thelifecentre.com

Narendra Mehta
136 Holloway Road, London N7 8DD
020 7609 3590
www.indianchampissage.com

Natalia and Terry O'Sullivan
01278 653 142
www.sacredhealers.co.uk

Penny Thornton
PO Box 534, Huntingdon PE29 9AX
www.astrolutely.com

Ravi Ponniah at Insight
Care Chapel Market
24 Chapel Market, London N1 9EZ
020 7278 1212

Rita Rogers
www.ritarogers.co.uk

Tristan Morell
6b Grange Road, Eastbourne
Sussex BN21 4EU
07866 266 997
www.tristanmorell.com

PARTY

151 Club
151 Kings Road, London SW3 5TX
0871 332 3202

Admiral Codrington
17 Mossop Street, London SW3 2LY
020 7581 0005
www.theadmiralcodrington.co.uk

Amika

65 Kensington High Street, London W8 5ED

0845 666 5001

www.amikalondon.com

Angels Fancy Dress

119 Shaftesbury Avenue, London WC2H 8AE

020 7836 5678

Annabel's

44 Berkeley Square, London W1J 5AR

020 7629 1096

Aragon House

247-249 New Kings Road

London SW6 4XG

020 7731 7313

www.aragonhouse.net

The Blue Bar

Berkeley Hotel, Wilton Place,

London SW1X 7RL

020 7235 6000

www.berkeleyhotellondon.com

Boujis

42 Thurloe Street, London SW7 2LQ

020 7584 2000

www.boujis.com

Brinkley's

47 Hollywood Road, Little Chelsea

London SW10 9HX

020 7351 1683

www.brinkleys.com

Builders Arms

13 Britten Street, London SW3 3TY

020 7349 9040

Capital VIP

www.capitalvip.com

Carpaccio

4 Sydney Street, London SW3 6PP

0207 352 3433

www.carpacciorestaurant.co.uk

Cat and Custard Pot

The Street, Shipton Moyne, Glos. GL8 8PN

01666 880 249

The Chelsea Flower Show

Royal Hospital, London SW3

020 7649 1885

www.rhs.org.uk

Chinawhite

6 Air Street, London W1B 5AA

0871 075 1734

www.chinawhite.com

Clouds
Clouds House, East Knoyle, Salisbury
Wilts SP3 6BE
01747 830 733
www.clouds.org.uk

Cowes Week
Regatta House, 18 Bath Road, Cowes,
Isle of Wight PO31 7QN
01983 295 744
www.skandiacowesweek.co.uk

The Cow
89 Westbourne Park Road, London W2 5QH
020 7221 0021
www.thecowlondon.co.uk

Crazy Homies
125 Westbourne Park Road, London W2 5QL
020 7727 6771
www.crazyhomieslondon.co.uk

The Cuckoo Club
Swallow Street, London W1B 4EZ
020 7287 4300
www.thecuckooclub.com

Cumberland Bar
1-3 Cumberland Street, Edinburgh EH3 6RT
01315 583 134
www.cumberlandbar.co.uk

Duke of Wellington
63 Eaton Terrace, London SW1W 8TR
020 7730 1782

E & O
14 Blenheim Crescent, London W11 1NN
020 7229 5454
www.ricker-restaurants.com

Eight over Eight
392 Kings Road, London SW3 5UZ
020 7349 9934
www.ricker-restaurants.com

The Electric
Electric House, 191 Portobello Road
London W11 2ED
020 7908 9696
www.the-electric.co.uk

Embassy Club
29 Old Burlington Street, London W1S 3AP
020 7851 0956
www.embassylondon.com

Essenza
210 Kensington Park Road, Notting Hill Gate
London W11 1NR
020 7792 1066
www.essenza.co.uk

Falklands Arms
Great Tew, Chipping Norton
Oxfordshire OX7 4DB
01608 683 653
www.falklandsarms.org.uk

La Famiglia
7 Langton Street, The Worlds End
Chelsea SW10 0JL
020 7351 0761
www.lafamiglia.co.uk

Foxtrot Oscar
79 Royal Hospital Road, London SW3 4HN
020 7352 7179

Glastonbury
www.glastonburyfestivals.co.uk

Goodwood
www.goodwood.co.uk

Griffin Inn
Fletching, Ickfield, Sussex TN22 3SS
01825 722 890
www.thegriffininn.co.uk

Hare and Hounds Hotel
Westonbirt, Tetbury, Glos. GL8 8QL
01666 881 000

Hedges & Butler
153 Regent Street, London W1B 4QB
020 7434 2232
www.hedgedandbutler.co.uk

Henley Royal Regatta
Regatta Headquarters, Henley-on-Thames,
Oxfordshire RG9 2LY
01491 572 153
www.hrr.co.uk

Hollywood Arms
45 Hollywood Road, London SW10 9HX
020 7349 7840
www.hollywoodarms.co.uk

Hoste Arms
The Green, Burnham Market, Kings Lynn,
Norfolk PE31 8HD
01328 738 777
www.hostearms.co.uk

Iglu
2b Jamaica Street, Edinbugh EH3 6HH
01314 765 333
www.theiglu.com

Kimberly Hall
www.kimberlyhall.net

Kitts
7-12 Sloane Square, London SW1W 8EQ
020 7881 5990
www.kitts-london.com

Ladbroke Arms
54 Ladbroke Road, London W11 3NW
020 7727 6648

The Lamb Inn
Hindon, Wilts SP3 6DP
01747 820 573
www.thelambathindon.co.uk

Lidgate's
110 Holland Park Avenue, London W11 4UA
020 7727 8243

Mahiki
1 Dover Street, London W1S 4LD
020 7493 9529
www.mahiki.com

Mamalanji
107 Kings Road, London SW3 4PA
020 7351 5521

Mariners Rock
Slipway, Rock, Cornwall PL27 6LD
01208 862 679
www.marinerrock.com

The Meadows
1655 N. Tegner Street, Wickenburg, AZ 85390
+1 928 684 3926
www.themeadows.org

Mo'vida
8-9 Argyll Street, London W1F 7TF
020 7734 5776
www.movida-club.com

Museum Inn
Farnham, Nr. Blandford Forum
Dorset DT11 8DE
01725 516 261
www.museuminn.co.uk

Non-Stop Party Shop
www.nonstopparty.co.uk

Notting Hill Arts Club
21 Notting Hill Gate, London W11 3JQ
020 7460 4459
www.nottinghillartsclub.com

Oyster Catcher
Polzeath, Cornwall PL27 6TG
01208 862 371

Party Planners
56 Ladbroke Grove, London W11 2PB
020 7229 9666
www.party-planners.co.uk

Pig's Ear
35 Old Church Street, London SW3 5BS
020 7352 2908
www.turningearth.co.uk

Portobello Road
London, W11
www.portobelloroad.co.uk

Quintessentially
www.quintessentially.com

Royal Ascot
Ascot Racecourse, Ascot, Berkshire, SL5 7JX
0870 727 1234
www.ascot.co.uk

The Secret Garden Party
www.secretgardenparty.com

Serena Cook
07780 633 225
www.deliciouslysortedibiza.com

The Ship Inn
41 Jews Row, London SW18 1TB
020 8870 9667

Summer Exhibition at the Royal Academy
Royal Academy of Arts
Burlington House, London W1J 0BD
020 7300 8000
www.royalacademy.org.uk

Star Inn
Harome, Nr. Helmsley, North Yorkshire
YO62 5JE
01439 770 397
www.thestaratharome.co.uk

The Supper Club
PO Box 688, London, SW3 4PJ
020 8968 3624
www.thesupperclublondon.com

The Tunnel House Inn
Tarlton Road, Coates, Glos. GL7 6PW
01285 770 2480

Verde Valley Guidance Clinic
8E Cottonwood Street, Cottonwood
Arizona 86326
+1 928 634 2236
www.verdevalleyguidanceclinic.com

The Victoria at Holkham
Park Road, Holkham
Norfolk NR23 1RG
01328 711 008
www.holkham.co.uk

The Vine Tree Inn
Randwick, Stroud, Glos. GL6 6JA
01453 763 748

Volstead
9 Swallow Street, London W1R 7HD
020 7287 1919
www.volstead.com

Wally Dug
32 Northumberland Street
Edinburgh EH3 6LS
01315 563 271

The Westbourne
101 Westbourne Park Villas, London W2 5ED
0207 221 1332
www.thewestbourne.com

The White Horse
1-3 Parson's Green, London SW6 4UL
020 7736 2115
www.whitehorsesw6.com

Wimbledon
The All England Lawn Tennis and Croquet Club,
Church Road, London SW19 5AE
020 8944 1066
www.wimbledon.org

Windsor Castle
Windsor SL4 1NJ
020 7766 7304
www.royalcollection.org.uk

OFF THE RAILS

**Alpha Course at the
Holy Trinity Brompton**
Brompton Road, London SW7 1JA
0845 644 7533
www.htb.org.uk/alpha

Capio Chelsea
1-5 Radnor Walk, London SW3 4PB
020 7349 3900
www.mentalhealth.capio.co.uk

Causeway
The Manor House, Ocea Island,
Essex SW3 4PB
020 7100 7260
www.1-1detox.co.uk/html/the_causeway.html

Champneys
Champneys Henlow Health Resort
The Grange, Henlow, SG16 6DB
08703 300 300
www.champneys.com

Clouds
Head Office, East Knoyle, Wilts SP3 6BE
01747 830 733
www.clouds.org.uk

Cottonwood
4110 W. Sweetwater Drive,
Tucson AZ 85745 USA
+1 520 7430411
www.cottonwooddetucson.com

Farm Place
Stane Street, Ockley, Surrey RH5 5NG
01306 627 742
www.prioryhealthcare.com

The Meadows
1655 N Tegher Street, Wickenberg AZ 85390
+1 928 684 3926
www.themeadows.org

Priory
Priory Hospital Roehampton,
Priory Lane, London SW15 5JJ
020 8876 8261
www.prioryhealthcare.co.uk

PROMIS Councelling Centre
10 Kendrick Mews, London SW7 3HG
020 7581 8222
www.promis.co.uk

PROMIS Recovery Centre
Pinners Hill, Nonington, Kent CT15 4LL
01304 841 700
www.promis.co.uk

Promises
Promises Treatment Centres
+1 866-390-2340

Weightwatchers
Millennium House,
Ludlow Road, Maidenhead, Berkshire SL6 2SL
www.weightwatchers.co.uk

PICTURE CAPTIONS AND CREDITS

INTRODUCTION
p. xv   Kate Middleton and her parents Carole and Michael, 2006 © Tim Graham/Getty Images
p. xxii   Boris Johnson and bunny girls at Viz 25th Anniversary party, 2004 © Getty Images

ECO SLOANE
p. 1   Anya Hindmarch shopping bag, 2007 © Mario Tama/Getty Images
p. 2   Eco Sloane illustration, 2007 © Sujean Rim
p. 3   Eco Sloane illustration, 2007 © Sujean Rim
p. 4   Eco Sloane baby illustration, 2007 © Sujean Rim
p. 7   Louise's Hunter Wellies, 2007 © Chris Shamwana
p. 8   Map of the United Kingdom, 2007 © Jiri Moucka/Shutterstock
p. 9   Piggy bank, 2007 © ryasick/Shutterstock
p. 10   David Cameron and Zac Goldsmith, 2005 © Bruno Vincent/Getty Images
p. 11   Prince Charles talks to Hugh Fearnley Whittingstall, 2004 © Martyn Hayhow/Getty Images
p. 12   Incense, 2007 © Matt Regan/Shutterstock
             Anya Hindmarch, 2006 © Dave M. Benett/Getty Images
             Moroccan slippers, 2007 © Gautier Willaume/Shutterstock
             Candles, 2007 © Claudia Cioncan/Shutterstock
p. 13   Elephant, 2007 © Norma Cornes/Shutterstock
p. 14   Zac Goldsmith, 2007 © Clive Rose/Getty Images
pp. 14-15   Red lips, 2007 © akva/Shutterstock
p. 16   Otis Ferry, 2006 © Mat Cardy/Getty Images
p. 18   Prince William visits his father's farm, 2004 © Anwar Hussein/Getty Images
p. 19   Eggs, 2007 © Zoran Djekic/Getty Images
p. 20   Vegetable and fruit basket, 2007 © Elena Elisseeva/Getty Images
p. 21   Carbon footprint, 2007 © kazberry/Shutterstock
p. 22   Eco Sloane baby illustration, 2007 © Sujean Rim
p. 23   Artichoke, 2007 © Shutterstock
p. 24   Pig, 2007 © Eric Isselée/Shutterstock
p. 25   Hugh Fearnley-Whittingstall, 2004 © David Levenson/Getty Images
p. 26   Market stall selling fruit, 2007 © David Hughes/Shutterstock
p. 27   Telesterion, 2007 © DEA/Getty Images
p. 28   Alternative fuel vehicle, 2005 © Scott Barbour/Getty Images
p. 29   Liberty Livelihood March, 2002 © Peter Glenser
p. 31   Master of the Hunt with fox hounds, 2007 © Jean Frooms/Shutterstock
p. 32   The Countryside March, 2002 © Peter Glenser
p. 33   The Connaught Square Squirrel Hunt, 2006 © Peter Glenser
p. 34   Young fox, 2007 © Art McKenzie/Shutterstock
p. 35   Shooting, 2005 © Peter Glenser
p. 36   Pheasant, 2007 © robynrg/Shutterstock
p. 37   'Would you like me to hold your cock?', 2005 © Bryn Parry
p. 38   Sloane Square, 2007 © Patrick Brice
p. 39   Rupert Everett, 2007 © Nick Harvey/Getty Images
p. 40   Sting and Bob Geldof, 2005 © David Levenson/Getty Images
p. 41   Anya Hindmarch shopping bag, 2007 © Mario Tama/Getty Images
p. 42   Invitation illustration, 2007 © C K Press

CHAV SLOANE
p. 43   Chihuahua, 2007 © Tyler Olson/Shutterstock

p. 44   Daniella Westbrook and her daughter, 2003 © Steve Finn/Getty Images
p. 45   Madonna and Guy Richie, 2007 © Jeff Vespa/Getty Images
p. 46   Chav Sloane illustration, 2007 © Sujean Rim
p. 47   Shoebox illustration, 2007 © Sujean Rim
p. 48   Manolo Blahnik Kanun shoe, 2007 © Manolo Blahnik
p. 49   Doughnuts, 2007 © StudioNewmarket/Shutterstock
p. 50-1 Photographers wait for Kate Middleton, 2007 © Gareth Cattermole/Getty Images
p. 52   Princess Diana, 1995 © Stringer/Getty Images
p. 53   Princess Diana, 1996 © Anwar Hussein/Getty Images
p. 54   Tara Palmer-Tomkinson, 2006 © Eric Ryan/Getty Images
p. 55   Tamara Beckwith, 2006 © Eric Ryan/Getty Images
p. 56   Lady Victoria Hervey, 2006 © Claire Greenway/Getty Images
p. 57   Clapper boards, 2007 © Studio Araminta/Shutterstock
p. 58   Big Brother 7 contestant George Askew, 2006 © Chris Jackson, Getty Images
p. 59   Susannah Constantine, Tamara Beckwith and Trinny Wodall, 2003 © Grazer Harrison/Getty Images
p. 60   (Top) P Diddy and friend, 2003 © Eric Ryan/Getty Images
p. 60   (Bottom) Joint of meat, 2007 © LockStockBob/Shutterstock
p. 61   Jules Holland, 2007 © Chris Jackson/Getty Images
p. 62   (Top) Prince Harry and Chelsy Davy, 2006 © MJ Kim/Getty Images
p. 62   (Bottom) Chihuahua, 2007 © Photomediacom/Shutterstock
p. 63   Bank notes, 2007 © Joe Gough/iStock
p. 64   Newspapers, 2007 © Paul Turner/Shutterstock
p. 65   (Top) Mobile phone, 2007 © Anna Sirotina
p. 65   (Bottom) The Kray brothers, 1965 © Ron Gerelli/Getty Images
p. 66   Terry Downes at the Thomas-A-Beckett Gym, 1957 © David E. Steen/Getty Images
p. 67   Wayne Rooney, 2006 © John Peters/Getty Images
p. 68   (Top) Kebabs, 2007 © Stephen Coburn/Shutterstock
p. 68   (Bottom) Dan Macmillan, 2006 © Dave M. Benett/Getty Images

THUMPING SLOANE
p. 69   Man pinioned by croquet hoop, 2006 © Peter Glenser
p. 70   Thumping Sloane illustration, 2006 © Sujean Rim
p. 73   Cresta Run building, 2007 © David Jack
p. 74   The Queen's Royal Lancers, 1993 © Tim Graham/Getty Images
p. 76   Dead pheasant, 2007 © Marilyn Barbone/Shutterstock
p. 78   Pamplona Bull Run, 2007 © A. Arrizurieta/Getty Images
p. 79   Man entering Ball, 2005 © Peter Glenser
p. 80   Milton Abbey, 1942 © David E. Scherman/Getty Images
p. 82   Oxford students celebrate May Day, 2005 © Bruno Vincent/Getty Images
p. 83   Man sliding down banister, 2005 © Peter Glenser
p. 84   David Kirke, 1987 © Terry Smith/Getty Images

SLEEK & EURO SLOANE
p. 85   Flower in water, 2007 © Ye/Shutterstock
p. 86   Sleek Sloane illustration, 2007 © Sujean Rim
p. 89   Jemima Khan, 2007 © Harold Cunningham/Getty Images
p. 90   Oxygen canister, 2007 © Greg McCracken/Shutterstock
p. 91   The Venus de Milo, 2007 © Hulton Archive/Getty Images
p. 93   Maurice Harold Macmillan with his wife Dorothy, c.1960 © Stringer/Getty Images
p. 95   Prince Charles with the Duchess of Cornwall leaving St.George's Chapel, 2005 © Alastair Grant/Getty Images
p. 96   Lady Diana Spencer with Camilla Parker-Bowles, 1980 © Express Newspapers/Getty Images
p. 98   Plum Sykes, 2007 © Dave M. Bennet/Getty Images

p. 162   Fire Island Ferry, 2007 © Ezra Shaw/Getty Images
p. 163   Cherie Blair, 2007 © Daniel Berekulak/Getty Images
p. 165   Bahima herdsman, Uganda, 1958 © George Rodger/Magnum Photos
p. 166   Juliette Binoche and Jish Noshi, 2005 © Dave M. Benett/Getty Images

PARTY SLOANE
p. 167   Boots at Glastonbury, 2007 © Rosie Greenway/Getty Images
p. 168   Party Sloane illustration, 2007 © Sujean Rim
p. 170   Mistletoe Ball, 2007 © Capital VIP
p. 173   Serpentine Summer Party, 2007 © Dave M. Benett/Getty Images
p. 174   Debutantes at the Queen Charlotte's Ball, 1950 © Keystone/Getty Images
p. 175   Betty Kenward , 1975 © Milton Wordley/Getty Images
p. 178   Woman with champagne, 2006 © Mike Sommer
p. 179   Solo rower, 2007 © Nikos/iStock
p. 181   R & R, 2006 © Matt Blakemore
p. 182   Ibiza harbour, 2007 © Styve Reinecke/Shutterstock
p. 183   James Blunt, 2005 © Djamilla Rosa Cohen/Getty Images
p. 184   P Diddy, 2003 © Eric Ryan/Getty Images
p. 185   Prince William and Kate Middleton leave Boujis, 2007 © Nat Travers/Getty Images
p. 186   Annabel's, 2007 © Stuart Wilson/Getty Images
p. 187   Pineapple with lei, 2007 © William Berry/Shutterstock
p. 188   Address books, 2007 © Chris Shamwana
p. 189   Capital VIP logo, 2007 © Capital VIP
p. 190   Party poppers, 2007 © bhathaway/Shutterstock
p. 191   Mischa Barton and friends at the Serpentine Summer Party, 2007 © Dave M. Benett/Getty Images
p. 192   Dollar sign necklace, 2007 © Scott Rothstein/Getty Images
p. 193   Lady Gabriella and Lord Frederick Windsor, 2007 © Tim Graham/Getty Images
p. 194   The Duke of Wellington, 2007 © Patrick Brice
p. 196   The Admiral Codrington, 2007 © The Admiral Codrington
p. 197   Tamsin Lonsdale, 2006 © Dave M. Benett/Getty Images
p. 198   Lord Frederick Windsor, 2005 © Dave M. Benett/Getty Images
p. 199   Blenheim Palace, 2005 © Tim Graham/Getty Images
p. 200   Lidgate's, 2005 © Lidgate Ltd.
p. 202   Ice Cream Van, 2005 © Toby Bradbury

SLOANE OFF THE RAILS
p. 203   'Too Far, Too Fast', 1900 © Arthur Trevena Collection
p. 204   Sloane Off the Rails illustration, 2007 © Sujean Rim
p. 206   Cross, 2007 © alva/Shutterstock
p. 207   Stained glass window, 2007 © Madeleine Openshaw/Shutterstock
p. 208   Tara Palmer-Tomkinson, 2003 © Dave M. Benett/Getty Images
p. 210   Prince Charles, 2007 © Matt Cardy/Getty Images
p. 211   Sarah Ferguson, 2006 © Katy Winn/Getty Images
p. 212   Sarah Ferguson, 2000 © David McNew/Getty Images
p. 213   Cartoon castle, 2007 © Holly Jones/Shutterstock
p. 214   James Hewitt, 2004 © Will Conran/Getty Images
p. 215   Camilla Parker-Bowles out with the Beaufort Hunt, 1998 © UK Press/Getty Images
p. 216   Prince Harry, 2005 © Anwar Hussein/Getty Images
p. 217   Tony Benn, 2003 © Cambridge Jones/Getty Images
p. 218   The Tower of London, 2007 © Kaspars Grinvalds/Shutterstock
p. 220   Tara Palmer-Tomkinson, 2002 © Tim Graham/Getty Images
p. 221   The Priory Clinic, 2006 © David Lodge/Getty Images
p. 222   The Meadows Clinic, 1999 © John Chapple/Getty Images

ACKNOWLEDGEMENTS

Ann Barr the original Dean of Sloane Studies at the University of Sloaneshire, who has worked tirelessly for this new branch of anthropology.

Cooler, Faster, More Expensive would not have been possible without the tireless efforts of those at Atlantic Books. Special heart-felt thanks go to Sarah Norman, Sarah Castleton, George Capel, Rebecca Winfield, and our Publisher Toby Mundy. To Jon Woods and Andy Chapman at five twentyfive, thank you for achieving the near impossible and to Chris Shamwana, Louise Brice, Patrick Brice and Alice Channer thank you for efforts above and beyond the call of duty. To Louisa and Olivia we will be eternally, sloanily, grateful.

This book has been created with contributions from Sloanes up and down the country. We are more grateful than we can say for their help and perfectly understand their desire for anonymity.